Extension

Mathematics

Tony Gardiner

alpha

OXFORD

UNIVERSITY PRESS

OXFORD
UNIVERSITY PRESS

Great Clarendon Street, Oxford OX2 6DP

Oxford University Press is a department of the University of Oxford.
It furthers the University's objective of excellence in research, scholarship,
and education by publishing worldwide in

Oxford   New York

Auckland   Cape Town   Dar es Salaam   Hong Kong   Karachi
Kuala Lumpur   Madrid   Melbourne   Mexico City   Nairobi
New Delhi   Shanghai   Taipei   Toronto

With offices in

Argentina   Austria   Brazil   Chile   Czech Republic   France   Greece
Guatemala   Hungary   Italy   Japan   Poland   Portugal   Singapore
South Korea   Switzerland   Thailand   Turkey   Ukraine   Vietnam

British Library Cataloguing in Publication Data

Data available

ISBN-13: 978 019 915 1509

10 9 8 7 6 5 4 3 2 1

Printed in Great Britain

Contents

Introduction

This is the first book in a series containing extension material designed for the top 25% or so of lower secondary pupils.

Good quality extension material is not specifically age-related: a good problem appeals to all ages – *as long as it is accessible*. Book *Alpha* is designed to be accessible to the top 25% or so of pupils in the first years of secondary school. I have tried to limit assumed prerequisite knowledge to what might be expected at some stage during Year 7 (age 11-12); *but it is in no way restricted to that age group*. The material is suitable for, and can be used effectively with, any able pupils in Years 7-9 to whom it is not already familiar, and some of the ideas may be directly relevant to certain older students. (In schools with higher levels of expectation, much of the material can no doubt be used with younger age-groups. However, since much of the material here seeks to encourage pupils not just to grind out answers, but to *think* and to talk about elementary techniques, there are good reasons for hesitating to use the material prematurely, even if at first sight it looks accessible. Nevertheless, teachers are encouraged to adapt and to use sections in ways the author never imagined!) Subsequent volumes are designed for those in School Years 8, 9, 10 and above.

The material uses the current English *Frameworks* as a guide. But – within this constraint – it seeks to capture and to convey *the essence of elementary mathematics*, rather than to reflect current expectations and norms.

Forty years ago England had a worldwide reputation for the way its schools extended able young mathematicians. This past reputation needs to be interpreted with caution. However, there is no escaping the fact that the structures *currently* in place *fail* to lay appropriate foundations for the most able 25%. Mathematics retains its perennial appeal – as shown by the huge expansion in mathematics competitions and other extra-curricular opportunities. Yet

◎ very few English Year 9 students achieve at the expected level for able pupils (as indicated by international comparisons)

◎ numbers choosing to study A level mathematics have slumped (despite repeated attempts to make the subject 'more accessible' by removing more demanding material)

◎ our leading universities find it increasingly difficult to identify suitable home-grown applicants who wish to study mathematics.

Mathematics at all levels begins when two or three elementary ideas have to be selected and combined – often in slightly unexpected ways – to solve an elementary but unfamiliar problem. An extension curriculum that embodies this principle is urgently needed – and not just for a small minority of pupils. It should be designed to establish a stronger foundation for a large fraction (around 25%) of each cohort, providing material suitable for *whole classes*, so giving teachers and senior management something to enrich the daily diet for *at least one top set* in every secondary school.

The range of ability between the 75th percentile and the 99th percentile is staggering. Hence the items presented here have been classified into three levels:

* *Tasters* (numbered **T1** etc.) are meant to be accessible to all pupils in the target group in the sense that they should all be able to tackle the problems and to have a degree of success (though some pupils will inevitably begin to struggle with the later problems, even on *Taster* sets).

* *Core* items (numbered **C1** etc.) cover curriculum topics relatively systematically, but may be appropriate only for a subset of those who engage with the *Tasters*. (How big this subset is will inevitably depend on the school and how the pupils have been taught.)

* *Extension* items (numbered **E1** etc.) push *Core* ideas slightly further, or venture a little beyond the official curriculum (whilst keeping their feet firmly on the ground).

Very roughly one might expect *Tasters* to be suitable for 25% of each cohort, *Core* to be suitable for 15-20%, and *Extensions* suitable for 5-10%; however, such figures are highly dependent on teachers' expectations. Complete answers (with additional discussion) are included in the associated *Teacher's Book*.

Each *Taster* and *Core* section includes a set of problems that is designed to encourage pupils to *develop a specific conceptual insight*, using material that is *closely related to what one finds in most mathematics classrooms*. The problems are to be actively tackled, and thought about – not merely 'answered'. Most prerequisites should have been covered in ordinary classwork. *Internal* prerequisites that might otherwise be overlooked are indicated at the top of the relevant section; obvious prerequisites (e.g. where the section title indicates a link with some earlier section – such as *Skittles B*, or *More angles*) are not mentioned explicitly. More general issues and connections are clarified in the associated *Teacher's Book*.

* Earlier sections are generally easier (in some sense) than later sections, but there is nothing to stop teachers selecting sections to suit their needs.

◎ The purpose of each section may be missed if pupils are allowed to produce answers in a way that is not in the intended spirit. In particular, the label 'NC' means 'No Calculators'.

◎ Each *Taster* and *Core* section is designed to be used with a complete class.
Every such section begins with **i** a short introductory text and **ii** a *Problem 0*.

  i The short introductory text in each section must be understood before pupils begin, but teachers are encouraged to decide for themselves how best to structure any necessary review.

  ii *Problem 0* is to be tackled by the whole class. Where this is done individually in the first instance, the results should subsequently be discussed as a group, with contributions and explanations orchestrated by the teacher *to bring out the intended spirit of the section*, and to emphasise any intended approach and layout indicated in the introductory text.

◎ *Problem 0* is *not* meant to be solved by the teacher as a 'worked example'. Rather it is to be solved *by the class* and should be used to bring out – and to correct – misconceptions and errors, so that every member of the class understands how to approach such problems, and so that all pupils emerge from the discussion with a clear idea of what is expected in that section.

◎ *Problem 0* often includes a harder part. This too is to be solved *by the class*, with explanations *from the class*, to ensure that everyone sees how the simple principles being developed can be used to solve harder problems.

◎ Each section requires one or more *specific* insights; any contributions during the preliminary class discussion that could obscure the intended focus need to be handled carefully. The *way* in which the problems are solved is crucial. Hence the initial class discussion needs to be handled in such a way as to ensure that pupils emerge with the necessary tools to tackle the problems that follow in the intended spirit.

Roughly speaking, my goal has been to pursue important themes from the official curriculum in ways that make mathematics more attractive, exploring simple ideas *more deeply*, and bringing out *connections between these simple ideas*. The existing curriculum should thereby be mastered in greater depth, with connections between topics being systematically established and exploited, counteracting the trend in recent years towards

i   increasing fragmentation

ii superficial coverage

• lack of fluency

• failure to develop a clear notion of mathematical proof

all of which contribute to a general failure to engage pupils' mathematical imagination.

Many able pupils are not used to tackling unfamiliar problems using only what they know. When they meet unfamiliar material, there may be pressure on the teacher to 'help' by giving rules that would reduce pupils' need to struggle. However, such premature rules prevent pupils developing their own habit of 'sense making', and deprive them of the satisfaction of achieving the relevant unexpected insight for themselves, and the experience of applying that insight to new problems.

Mathematical mastery requires a considerable amount of repetitive exercising of simple processes. Repetitive practice is needed to achieve the level of *fluency* and *accuracy* that will allow longer chains of calculation to be completed without introducing unanticipated errors due to 'overload'. Such repetition can be a source of considerable pleasure and satisfaction for the learner (and often involves a greater degree of challenge than we acknowledge). Most sections in this series contain lots of exercises to provide this kind of repetition-with-a-purpose.

But it is also important that basic techniques should be routinely used to solve more demanding problems. Thus most *Taster* and *Core* sections include a number of problems of a more demanding kind; such problems sometimes appear in a shaded box . These problems are not necessarily harder, or intended for a minority; the shaded box is simply an indication that these problems may require a greater degree of thought.

Extension sections provide additional (mostly harder) problems, mainly for those pupils who have already devoured the *Taster* and *Core* sections and who need something more demanding. The *Extension* sections differ slightly from the *Taster* and *Core* sections: whereas the *Taster* and *Core* sections are designed to be used with whole classes, and so have a clear structure, the *Extension* sections may be appropriate only for a minority of those in a top set; so it seems counterproductive to prescribe how they should be used. Each section has a theme – but the focus is slightly blurred to keep pupils on their toes. Later problems in each section still tend to be harder than earlier problems; but *Extension* sections are less systematic about highlighting more demanding problems by including them in a shaded box. These sections should therefore be seen as an extra resource in the spirit of *Taster* and *Core* sections, to be used as teachers and pupils see fit.

Elementary mathematics retains its unrivalled potential to appeal to young minds. But many essential techniques and attitudes have recently been downplayed or neglected. This neglect stems in part from pressure on schools to demonstrate 'success' in narrowly focused, and increasingly predictable, central assessments. Unfortunately, tests which are obliged to demonstrate success shy away from those aspects of elementary mathematics that appeal to young minds precisely because they are *accessible, but slightly elusive*. But as observed above, mathematics proper begins when two or three elementary ideas need to be combined to solve an unfamiliar problem. *This series of books provides problem sequences that aim to reinstate this experience on a very simple level.*

◎ The material requires pupils who are willing to struggle, to experience discomfort, and who come to accept this as 'normal' (even tantalising).

◎ In each section *Problem 0* (tackled by the class under the guidance of the teacher) provides the opportunity for any necessary review and preparation.

Pupils may still feel uncomfortable when confronted with the need to work quickly and accurately, or to make sense of unfamiliar-looking problems, but this activity is quintessentially human, and – provided that the demands being made are not unrealistic – the result for ordinary pupils can only be positive. In particular, one can anticipate a fresh flexibility, self-criticism, and self-correction when the same pupils are faced with more straightforward tasks.

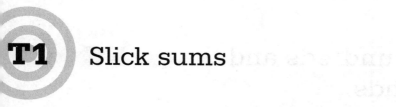

T1 Slick sums

NC

Two aspects of arithmetic help to make calculations easier than they look.

◎ The first is the way we write numbers – with *units*, *tens* and *hundreds*. This makes it much easier to think about large numbers – since 74 is just '7 *tens* and 4 *units*' rather than 'seventy-four dots'.

◎ The second is the 'laws of arithmetic'.
   For example, we can add up a list of numbers in the most convenient order (so long as we don't leave any out, or count some more than once).

Use these two ideas to work out the additions and subtractions below as simply as you can. Don't just grind out the answers; stay alert and *think!*

Problem 0

0 a	73 + 48 + 27 =	
b	213 – 169 + 170 =	
c	654 – 398 + 397 =	

1 37 + 96 – 37 =   **7** 132 – 59 + 28   =

2 37 + 96 + 63 =   **8** 76 + 39 + 14   =

3 64 + 73 – 71 =   **9** 76 + 49 – 26   =

4 52 – 37 + 15 =   **10** 243 – 159 + 158 =

5 81 – 47 + 49 =   **11** 138 – 50 + 112 =

6 79 + 83 – 80 =

2 Work out the answers to these as efficiently as you can.

a 133 – 48 + 17 – 102 =

b 302 – 29 – 271 =

c 181 – 182 + 183 – 184 + 185 – 186 + 187 – 188 + 189 =

T2 Tens, hundreds and thousands   NC

Our place value system for writing numbers is based on 10s, 100s, 1000s, and so on. This makes some multiplications especially important.

Work out $2 \times 5 \quad = \underline{}$
$2 \times 50 \quad = \underline{}$ $4 \times 25 \quad = \underline{}$ $5 \times 20 \quad = \underline{}$
$2 \times 500 = \underline{}$ $4 \times 250 = \underline{}$ $5 \times 200 = \underline{}$
$20 \times 50 = \underline{}$ $25 \times 40 = \underline{}$ $8 \times 125 = \underline{}$

Problem 0

> **0** Sometimes an awkward-looking multiplication is easier than it looks because one of the above multiplication facts is hidden inside it. Work these three out *in your head*.
>
> **a** $15 \times 20 = (\underline{} \times 5) \times 20 = \underline{} \times (5 \times 20) =$
>
> **b** $12 \times 75 = (\underline{} \times 4) \times (25 \times \underline{}) =$
>
> **c** $375 \times 8 =$

Use the ideas in problem **0** to work out the answers to these multiplications *in your head*.

1 $16 \times 25 =$ **9** $75 \times 16 =$

2 $25 \times 40 =$ **10** $35 \times 14 =$

3 $65 \times 20 =$ **11** $12 \times 75 =$

4 $12 \times 25 =$ **12** $175 \times 16 =$

5 $15 \times 12 =$ **13** $75 \times 36 =$

6 $75 \times 8 =$ **14** $125 \times 16 =$

7 $15 \times 16 =$ **15** $375 \times 8 =$

8 $35 \times 40 =$ **16** $225 \times 40 =$

> **17** Use the same idea to work out the answers to these multiplications in your head.
>
> **a** $75 \times 28 = \underline{}$ **c** $625 \times 32 = \underline{}$
>
> **b** $375 \times 48 = \underline{}$ **d** $875 \times 56 = \underline{}$

Calculating is a bit like cooking a simple meal: the ingredients are given; you then have to combine them correctly and follow the recipe.

Mathematics is more than calculation: you need to be able to calculate quickly and accurately, but you also need to learn to be flexible and to work backwards like a detective, that is,

> you are given an outcome (or a meal already prepared),
> and you have to work out how it arose (or what went into it).

Problem 0

> **0** Three monkeys eat a total of 15 nuts. Each monkey eats an odd number of nuts.
>
> **a** Suppose that each monkey eats more than one nut, and that no two monkeys eat the same number of nuts.
> How many nuts does each monkey eat?
> How many different solutions are there?
>
> **b** Suppose that all you know is that each monkey eats more than one nut.
> How many different solutions would there be then?

To find all possible solutions without missing any, there is little point just trying numbers to see if they work; you need a *method*.

One way of organising your search is to consider the *least greedy* monkey first.

> Average number of nuts per monkey = ___.

In problem **0a**, each monkey eats an o** number of nuts bigger than 1, and no two monkeys eat the same number of nuts.

∴ Each monkey eats an o** number of nuts ≥ ___ .

∴ There is just ___ possibility for the least greedy monkey.

Now consider in turn all possibilities for the *second smallest number*.

1 Tripods have three legs; Bipods have two legs. Some Tripods and Bipods have 15 legs altogether.

   i   How many Tripods are there?

   ii How many Bipods are there?

2 Three birds laid 15 eggs between them. Each bird laid an odd number of eggs.

   i   If no two birds laid the same number of eggs, how many eggs did each bird lay?

   ii How many different solutions are there?

3 a Some Tripods and Bipods – at least two of each – have 23 legs altogether.
     How many Tripods are there?
     How many Bipods are there?

   b Some Tripods and Bipods have 23 legs altogether, but you know nothing about how many of each there are.
     What additional solutions could there be?

4 In a fairground shooting gallery each target I hit has a score which is an integer. My three shots all scored, all three scores were different, and each score was an even number. My total was 18.

   a What can you say about my lowest score?

   b How many different solutions are there?

5 When playing mini-cricket in the back garden a *boundary* scores either 3 or 4. I hate running, so I try to score all my runs in boundaries, with at least one boundary of each kind.
What is the smallest score that can be achieved like this in two different ways?

T4 Intelligent grouping NC

You know that '3 *chairs* and 7 *chairs* make (3 + 7 =) 10 *chairs*'.

But you might sometimes forget that this works for all kinds of 'objects'.

In particular, if you group things in *tens*, then
'3 *tens* and 7 *tens* make 10 *tens* (or 1 hundred)'.

And if you group things in *eights*, then
'3 *eights* and 7 *eights* make 10 *eights* (or 80)'
that is, $(3 \times 8) + (7 \times 8) = (3 + 7) \times 8$
$$= 10 \times 8 = 80$$

Use this idea to answer each question *quickly in your head* (that is, without working out the two brackets separately and then adding).

Problem 0

0 a $(14 \times 7) - (2 \times 14) =$

  b $(7 \times 8) + (6 \times 4) \quad =$

1 $(13 \times 8) - (3 \times 8) = \underline{\hspace{1cm}} \times 8 =$ **6** $(13 \times 6) + (7 \times 6) \quad =$

2 $(14 \times 7) - (4 \times 7) =$ **7** $(6 \times 27) + (6 \times 3) \quad =$

3 $(13 \times 7) + (7 \times 7) =$ **8** $(4 \times 17) + (6 \times 17) =$

4 $(13 \times 8) + (7 \times 8) =$ **9** $(7 \times 19) + (19 \times 3) =$

5 $(23 \times 6) - (3 \times 6) =$

10 Now try these.

  a $(17 \times 12) + (13 \times 12) =$ **e** $(12 \times 14) + (6 \times 32) \quad =$

  b $(14 \times 15) + (15 \times 16) =$ **f** $(22 \times 26) + (6 \times 13) \quad =$

  c $(83 \times 7) + (17 \times 7) \quad =$ **g** $(23 \times 51) + (31 \times 17) =$

  d $(6 \times 67) + (33 \times 6) \quad =$

T5 Perimeters

The word *perimeter* is sometimes used to denote the outer edge, or boundary, of a two-dimensional figure. In mathematics it means the *length* of the outer edge.

The figures in this section are either triangles, or are made from rectangles. So if an angle *looks like* a right angle, you may assume that it *is* a right angle.

Problem 0

> **0 a** An isosceles triangle has perimeter 35.3 cm and base of length 10.9 cm.
>   How long are the other two sides?
>
> **b** Find the perimeter of the *two-step* shape shown below.
>
>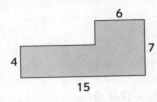
>
> Find the area of the shape.

1 I need special edging strip to go round the edge of a triangular lawn with sides of lengths 30 m, 40 m, and 45 m.
What length of edging do I need?

2 A triangle has sides of lengths 2.3 cm, 31 mm and 0.018 m.
Find its perimeter

   a in mm   **b** in cm   **c** in m.

3 A square has perimeter 10 m 52 cm.
How long is each side?

4 A rectangular field measures 42 m by 27 m.
What length of fence do I need to surround the field completely?

5 Find the perimeter of the *two-step* shape shown below.

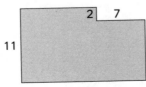

6 I draw a 4 cm by 4 cm square and then add internal lines to turn it into a 1 cm by 1 cm grid.
What is the total length (in cm) of *all* the lines in my diagram?

7 The six-step staircase shape shown on the right has base of length 15 cm and height 12 cm.
Find the perimeter of the shape.

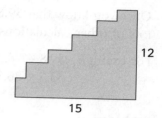

8 The six-step staircase shape shown on the right has base of length 12 cm and height 15 cm.
Find the perimeter of the shape.

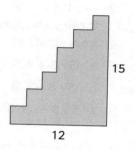

9 a The four-step staircase shape shown on the right has base of length 8 cm and height 6 cm.
Find the perimeter of the shape.

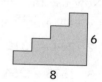

b Two copies of the four-step staircase shape in part **a** are fitted together.
Find the perimeter of the resulting shape.

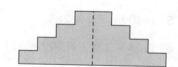

10 The shape shown here is obtained by cutting different staircase shapes from each corner of a 17 cm by 17 cm square.

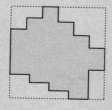

What are the possible values of the perimeter of the resulting shape?

Once you know that **59.8 − 26.3 = 33.5** you should be able to work out lots of other calculations *in your head*.

For example, '59.8 − 26.3 = 33.5' is just another way of saying
33.5 + 26.3 = 59.8, or 598 − 263 = 335, and so on.

Problem 0

0 Use the answer to the sum above to work out the answers to these sums purely by *thinking* (not by working out each one from scratch)!

  a (59.8 + 6.5) − 26.3 =   **d** (59.8 + 2.4) − (26.3 + 2.4)   =

  b (59.8 − 3.5) − 26.3 =   **e** (5.98 − 0.6) − (2.63 + 0.4)   =

  c 59.8 − (26.3 + 3.5) =   **f** (0.598 + 0.044) − (0.335 + 0.007) =

1 Work out the answer to 264 + 1309 = ___ in any way you like.

Now use the answer to this problem to calculate answers to problems **2-15** quickly, purely by *thinking*.

2 264 + 1310

3 1573 − (264 + 2)

4 263 + 1309

5 (1309 − 73) + 264

6 (264 + 17) + (1309 + 13)

7 262 + 1308

8 (1309 − 17.3) + (264 + 17.3)

9 26.4 + 130.9

10 1.573 − 1.309

11 157.3 − (26.4 + 0.9)

12 0.1309 + (0.0264 + 0.0027)

13 2000 − 1309 + 1573

14 400 − 264 + 1573

15 13.09 + 2.64

16 a (1573 − 17.3) − (1309 − 17.3) =

  b 1573 − (1309 + 24)   =

  c 1573 − (1309 − 36)   =

17 Work out 9494 − 1616 = ___ .
Use the answer to find quick answers to these calculations.

  a (94.94 + 0.24) − (16.16 + 0.02) =

  b (78.78 + 6.06) + 16.16   =

  c 0.1616 + (0.0006 + 0.7878)   =

Suppose I tell you to
'fill in the box to make this equation correct: $6 \times 25 = 3 \times$ ___ '

◎ You could do it *the hard way,* by
first working out $\qquad 6 \times 25 = 150$
and then realising that $\qquad 150 = 3 \times \underline{50}$

◎ But it is easier (and more sensible)
to take a factor 3 out of the 6, and rearrange the 'brackets'
$6 \times 25 = \underline{3 \times 2} \times 25 = 3 \times \underline{2 \times 25} = 3 \times \underline{50}$.

Use the second method to work out *in your head* what goes in
each space.

Problem 0

> **0 a** $49 \times 6 = 2 \times$ ___
>
> **b** $56 \times 125 = 7 \times$ ___
>
> **c** Sometimes you may have to 'steal' from both factors
> $46 \times 150 = 100 \times$ ___

1 $6 \times 8 = 2 \times$ ___   **8** $15 \times 16 = 4 \times$ ___

2 $8 \times 6 = 3 \times$ ___   **9** $12 \times 7 = 3 \times$ ___

3 $6 \times 8 = 4 \times$ ___   **10** $15 \times 16 = 5 \times$ ___

4 $15 \times 16 = 2 \times$ ___   **11** $12 \times 7 = 2 \times$ ___

5 $12 \times 7 = 6 \times$ ___   **12** $15 \times 16 = 6 \times$ ___

6 $15 \times 16 = 3 \times$ ___   **13** $9 \times 125 = 15 \times$ ___

7 $12 \times 7 = 4 \times$ ___   **14** $12 \times 75 = 10 \times$ ___

15 Use the same idea to work out the answers to these
multiplications in your head.

     a $35 \times 60 =$ **b** $75 \times 36 =$ **c** $125 \times 24 =$

16 A man packs 20 boxes with 18 peaches in each box. How
many boxes would he need if there were only 12 peaches in
each box?

You may have learned a different method, but multiplication is best done in column form – with units, tens and hundreds columns lined up.

For example, to calculate 23×649, write

$$
\begin{array}{r}
6\ 4\ 9 \\
\times \quad 2\ 3 \\
\hline
1\ 9\ 4\ 7 \\
1\ 2\ 9\ 8\ 0 \\
\hline
1\ 4\ 9\ 2\ 7 \\
\end{array}
$$

First multiply the units: $3 \times 649 = 1947$
Then multiply the tens: $20 \times 649 = 12\,980$
making sure that you enter the digits of your answer
in the correct column.

Finally, add the two parts to get the *answer*.

Work out these multiplications in the same way. Do *not* use a calculator.

Problem 0

0 Fill in the missing digits in the long multiplication below.

$$
\begin{array}{r}
6\ 4\ 9 \\
\times \quad 3\ 7 \\
\hline
4\ \square\ 4\ \square \\
\square\ 9\ \square\ \square\ 0 \\
\hline
\square\ \square\ \square\ \square\ \square \\
\end{array}
$$

1 148×3 =

2 143×7 =

3 $303 \times 22 =$

4 77×13 =

5 91×11 =

6 429×21 =

7 $3003 \times 37 =$

8 $533 \times 231 =$

9 Work out the missing digits in these multiplications.

a
$$
\begin{array}{r}
\square\ 7\ \square \\
\times \quad \square\ 3 \\
\hline
\square\ 1\ \square\ 9 \\
\square\ \square\ \square\ 4\ \square \\
\hline
\square\ \square\ \square\ \square\ \square \\
\end{array}
$$

b
$$
\begin{array}{r}
\square\ 7 \\
\times \quad \square\ \square \\
\hline
4\ \square\ \square \\
\square\ \square\ 6\ \square \\
\hline
\square\ \square\ \square\ 3 \\
\end{array}
$$

T9 Angles

Geometrical diagrams use a special 'language'.
Right angles are marked like this:

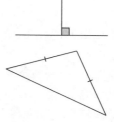

If you know that two line segments (e.g. two sides of a
particular triangle) are equal, then you can mark them
both in the same way – say with a dash as in this triangle.

If you know *some* of the angles in a
geometrical figure, you can often work out
other angles exactly – using these *four basic facts*.

◉ Angles at a point on a straight line add to ___°.

◉ Vertically opposite angles are ___ .

◉ The two 'base angles' of any isosceles triangle
are ___ .

◉ The three angles in any triangle add to ___°.

Problem 0

0 One right angle is marked in the figure shown.
Your job is to work out the unknown angles *x*, *y* and *z*.

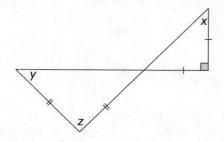

a How big is the angle marked *x*?

b How big is the angle marked *y*?

c How big is the angle marked *z*?

Use the given information to work out the angles marked with letters.

1

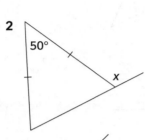

40°

x

2

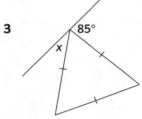

50°

x

3

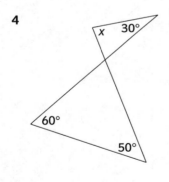

85°

x

4

x 30°

60°

50°

5

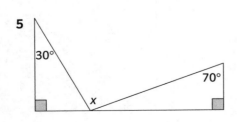

30°

70°

x

6

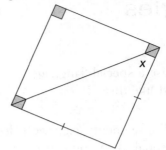

x

7

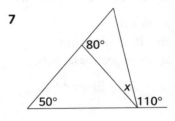

80°

50°

x

110°

8

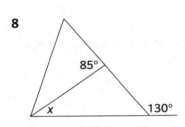

85°

x

130°

9

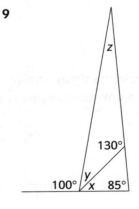

z

130°

y

100° x 85°

10

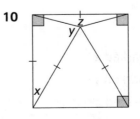

z

y

x

 **T10** Cunning calculation *A* **NC**

or each of the four basic operations of arithmetic there is a *standard algorithm* that works in all cases. You should be completely fluent n implementing these standard algorithms efficiently and accurately. ut it is also important to have an understanding of place value that llows you to remain flexible in case there may be simpler ways of alculating.

ry to see why each of these sums has been broken down in a particular vay, and use this insight to complete the calculation in your head.

roblem 0

0 a $5327 + 97 = (5324 + 3) + 97 = 5324 + \_\_\_ =$

   b $43.5 - 12.4 = (42.4 + 1.1) - 12.4 = \_\_\_ + 1.1 =$

1 $5643 + 489 = (5632 + 11) + 489 = 5632 + \_\_\_ =$

2 $60\,419 + 897 = (60\,416 + 3) + 897 = 60\,416 + \_\_\_ =$

3 $12\,345 - 678 = (12\,367 - 22) - 678 = 12\,367 - \_\_\_ =$

4 $304 + 2684 = (300 + 4) + 2684 = 300 + \_\_\_ =$

5 $487 + 3755 = \_\_\_ + (13 + 3542) = \_\_\_ + 3542 =$

6 $9636 - 3482 = (9636 + 18) - (3482 + 18) = 9654 - \_\_\_ =$

7 $41.3 - 12.4 = (42.4 - 1.1) - 12.4 = 42.4 - \_\_\_ =$

8 $123.6 - 14.8 = (124.8 - \_\_\_) - 14.8 =$

9 $233.6 - 14.8 = (233.6 + 5.2) - \_\_\_ =$

0 $75.4 - 9.7 = (79.7 - \_\_\_) - 9.7 =$

1 $175.4 - 9.7 = (175.4 + 0.3) - \_\_\_ =$

2 $125 \times 44 = 125 \times (4 \times 11) = \_\_\_ \times 11 =$

3 $225 \times 36 = 225 \times (4 \times \_\_\_) = \_\_\_ \times 9 =$

4 $75 \times 52 = 75 \times (\_\_\_ \times 13) = \_\_\_ \times 13 =$

5 $175 \times 72 = 175 \times (\_\_\_ \times 18) = \_\_\_ \times 18 =$

6 $375 \times 144 = (3 \times \_\_\_) \times (\_\_\_ \times 18) =$

7 $625 \times 144 = (25 \times 25) \times (\_\_\_ \times 9) = \_\_\_ \times 9 =$

T11 Drawing conclusions *A*

These tasks are designed partly to develop accuracy in drawing, and partly for the satisfaction of producing pleasing diagrams. However, the main goal is for you to *think about the mathematics behind the constructions.*

Problem 0

0 a Draw a circle with centre *O* and radius about 10 cm.
Mark two points *A* and *B* on the circle. Join *OA*, *OB*, *AB*.

  i Without measuring, what can you say about ∠*OAB* and ∠*OBA*? Explain your answer.

  ii Measure ∠*OAB*. Measure ∠*OBA*.

b i Draw a line segment *AB* 12 cm long.

  ii Use a protractor to mark a point *X* such that ∠*BAX* = 60°. Use a protractor to mark a point *Y* on the same side of *AB* as *X*, such that ∠*ABY* = 60°.

  iii Draw *AX* and *BY*; let these two lines (extended if necessary) cross at the point *C*.

  iv Without measuring, decide what you know about ∠*ACB*. Explain your answer. Measure ∠*ACB*.

  v Without measuring, what can you predict about the length of *AC*? What can you predict about the length of *BC*? Measure *AC* and *BC*.

The construction in problem **0a** depends on the basic property of i∗o∗∗e∗e∗ triangles.

The construction in problem **0b** may seem similar, but it is different: in problem **0a** you constructed a triangle with two equal *sides,* but in problem **0b** you constructed a triangle with two equal *angles.*
That these two properties *for triangles* turn out to be connected is not at all obvious – as one sees in problem **1** (about *parallelograms*).

 1 Suppose you are required to construct a parallelogram *ABCD*.

  a If the two adjacent *sides* *AB* and *AD* are equal, what does this tell you about the quadrilateral *ABCD*?

  b If the two adjacent *angles* ∠*ABC* and ∠*BAD* are equal, what does this tell you about the quadrilateral *ABCD*?

There are two separate parts to any construction:

   i   the procedure being followed

   ii the way you carry out that procedure.

Because eyes, fingers and pencils are imperfect, the implementation of stage **ii** is inevitably *approximate*.

What matters mathematically is whether the first part **i** (that is, *the procedure being followed*) is also approximate, or whether it is *exact in principle*.

The construction in problem **0b** follows a procedure involving measuring with a ruler and a protractor, and measurements, such as '12 cm', or '60°', are by their nature *approximate*.

In contrast, the procedure underlying the construction in the next problem is *exact*, even though the way you or I may implement that procedure is inevitably approximate.

2 Given any line segment *AB*, draw the circle *C* with centre *A* and passing through the point *B*, and the circle *C'* with centre *B* and passing through the point *A*. Let these two circles cross at *C* and *D*.

  a Without measuring, what do you *know* about the line segments *AB* and *AC*?
     Explain your answer.

  b Without measuring, what do you *know* about the line segments *BA* and *BC*?
     Explain your answer.

  c So what do you *know* about the triangle *ABC*?
     And what does this tell you about the three angles ∠*ABC*? ∠*BCA*? ∠*CAB*?
     Explain your answer.

The next problem involves drawing an angle of 90°, so it is inevitably approximate. However, you will learn, in due course, how to construct a perpendicular by a method that is *exact in principle*. What is mathematically (and educationally) interesting about the construction in problem **3** is that, while you may be certain in your own mind that the quadrilateral *ABCD* has certain properties, you may at this stage have difficulty *proving* this.

3 a Draw a line segment *AB* of length 10 cm.

b Use a protractor to construct a point *X* such that $\angle BAX = 90°$, and a point *Y* on the same side of *AB* as *X* such that $\angle ABY = 90°$.

c Draw the line *AX* and the line *BY*.

d Draw the circle with centre *A* through the point *B*; let this circle meet the line *AX* at the point *D*.
Draw the circle with centre *B* through the point *A*; let this circle meet the line *BY* at the point *C*.

e Draw the line *DC*.

f What do you expect to be true of the quadrilateral *ABCD*?

g Some properties of *ABCD* are fairly clear, but others are less obvious. For example, you should be able to explain why *AB*, *AD*, *BC* are all equal.

But it is probably not at all clear why *DC* should be the same length as *AB*. Try to fill in the details in the following proof.
Proof
$\angle BAD$ and $\angle ABC$ are both *i*** a***e*.
This guarantees that $\angle ADC + \angle BCD = \_\_\_°$.
So if you only know that $\angle ADC = \angle BCD$, then you can be sure that all four angles are *i*** a***e*.

Join *AC* and *BD*.

Explain why $\triangle ABD$ and $\triangle BAC$ are *congruent*.
Conclude that
i $AC = BD$ **ii** $\angle ADB = \angle BCA$.

Now explain why $\triangle BDC$ and $\triangle ACD$ are *congruent*.
Conclude that $\angle BDC = \angle ACD$.

$\therefore \angle ADC = \angle ADB + \angle BDC$
$\qquad = \angle\_\_\_ + \angle\_\_\_ = \angle BCD.$ **QED**

 **T12** Turning the tables NC

TASTER

If you know your tables, you should be able to see immediately what number to put in each space to make these equations correct.

___ ÷ 2 = 10

6 ÷ ___ = 2

Decide what number goes in the space to make each equation correct.

Problem 0

0 a ___ ÷ 6 = 8

b 72 ÷ ___ = 4

1 ___ ÷ 5 = 3

2 ___ ÷ 4 = 6

3 28 ÷ ___ = 4

4 54 ÷ ___ = 6

5 36 ÷ ___ = 4

6 ___ ÷ 7 = 11

7 ___ ÷ 8 = 9

8 56 ÷ ___ = 8

9 63 ÷ ___ = 7

10 42 ÷ ___ = 6

11 91 ÷ ___ = 7

12 68 ÷ ___ = 4

25

T13 Misplaced digits   NC

The idea of *Misplaced digits* was originally inspired by Eric Emmett (*Puffin Book of Brainteasers*, long since out of print), who had a wonderful character called Uncle Bungle. Uncle Bungle regularly got things wrong, but in a controlled way so that you could correct his mistakes!

Problem 0

> **0 a** The multiplication '$6 \times 2 = 3$' is clearly not quite right; but it is close! The digits are correct, the operation '$\times$' is correct, and the 'shape' of the sum ('one digit times one digit equals one digit') is correct; but the digits are in the wrong place.
>
> It should be: $2 \times 3 = 6$.
>
> Here is another multiplication: the digits are correct; the operation is correct; the shape is correct, but all the digits are in the wrong place.
> Can you fix it?
> $97 \times 5 = 31$
>
> **b** The addition on the right uses the digits 0 to 6 once each, but something is clearly wrong: the digits are all correct, the operation is correct and the shape of the sum is correct, but the digits are in the wrong places.
> Can you put it right?
>
> $$\begin{array}{r} 6\,5 \\ +\ 4\,3 \\ \hline 2\,1\,0 \\ \hline \end{array}$$

1   In each of these multiplications all the digits are correct, the operation is correct, and the shape of the sum is correct, but the digts are in the wrong places.
Can you fix them?

   a $17 \times 7 = 71$ **c** $47 \times 9 = 18$ **e** $34 \times 9 = 22$

   b $28 \times 1 = 44$ **d** $43 \times 2 = 14$ **f** $76 \times 8 = 41$

2   In these additions the digits are all correct, the operation is correct, and the shape of the sum is correct, but the digits are in the wrong places.
Can you fix them?

  a $\begin{array}{r} 1\,1 \\ +\,3\,3 \\ \hline 4\,8\,8 \\ \hline \end{array}$ **b** $\begin{array}{r} 9\,1 \\ +\,9\,1 \\ \hline 8\,9\,1 \\ \hline \end{array}$ **c** $\begin{array}{r} 1\,0 \\ +\,1\,8 \\ \hline 2\,8\,2 \\ \hline \end{array}$ **d** $\begin{array}{r} 3\,2 \\ +\,1\,7 \\ \hline 4\,9\,0 \\ \hline \end{array}$

3 a This addition is clearly wrong, but not hopelessly wrong.
Every digit is exactly one out.
Can you put it right?

$$\begin{array}{r} 6\,3\,2\,3 \\ +\,9\,6\,0\,6 \\ \hline 2\,3\,2\,5\,6 \end{array}$$

b This is just like the sum in part **a**: every digit is one out.
But this time it is a *subtraction*.
Can you put it right?

$$\begin{array}{r} 2\,1\,6\,6\,4\,8 \\ -\,9\,0\,1\,3\,5 \\ \hline 1\,3\,7\,8\,0 \end{array}$$

4 a This multiplication looks correct. But in fact every digit
is one out.
Can you work out the original sum without using
guesswork?

$$\begin{array}{r} 1\,6 \\ \times\,4 \\ \hline 6\,4 \end{array}$$

b These are just like the calculation in part **a**, except that they
have may more than one solution. Try to work out all solutions
in each case – again without using guesswork.

i
$$\begin{array}{r} 3\,4 \\ \times\,6 \\ \hline 2\,0\,4 \end{array}$$

ii
$$\begin{array}{r} 2\,5\,2 \\ \times\,6 \\ \hline 1\,5\,1\,2 \end{array}$$

iii
$$\begin{array}{r} 6\,7\,8 \\ \times\,5 \\ \hline 1\,2\,4\,5 \end{array}$$

c This is like the calculation in part **a** in that
every digit is one out.
But this time it is a *division*.
Can you put it right?

$$\begin{array}{r} 2\,9 \\ 8\,4\,\overline{)\,2\,2\,2\,3} \\ 6\,2 \\ \hline 6\,9\,3 \\ 4\,9\,3 \\ \hline \end{array}$$

d Here are two more divisions where every digit is one out.
Put them right.

i
$$\begin{array}{r} 3\,8 \\ 2\,3\,\overline{)\,8\,7\,5} \\ 7\,7 \\ \hline 2\,1\,5 \\ 4\,1\,5 \\ \hline \end{array}$$

ii
$$\begin{array}{r} 3\,4 \\ 1\,4\,\overline{)\,6\,1\,8} \\ 5\,5 \\ \hline 7\,8 \\ 5\,8 \\ \hline \end{array}$$

5 In these divisions the digits are all correct, but they are in the
wrong places.
Can you put them right?

a
$$\begin{array}{r} 2\,2 \\ 3\,3\,\overline{)\,6\,8\,8} \end{array}$$

b
$$\begin{array}{r} 5\,7 \\ 5\,3\,\overline{)\,2\,9\,4} \end{array}$$

T14 Percentages

NC

Percentages are not numbers: they are *operators*, or multipliers, or
scale factors. You can't have a percentage all on its own – you have to
have a percentage *of* some quantity.

Problem 0

0 a 25 % of 360 =

b 20 % of 85 =

c 65 % of 40 = $\dfrac{65}{100} \times 40 = \dfrac{\square}{20} \times 40 =$

25 % of 360 is defined to be

$$\frac{25}{100} \times 360 = \frac{1}{4} \times 360 = \underline{\quad}$$

1 75 % of 40 =   **6** 40 % of 45 =

2 40 % of 75 =   **7** 55 % of 65 =

3 55 % of 60 =   **8** 125 % of 24 =

4 45 % of 40 =   **9** 24 % of 125 =

5 60 % of 55 =

Since percentages are multipliers, there is nothing to stop us working
out a *percentage of a percentage* of a given quantity.

10 40 % of 50 % of 60 =   **14** 30 % of 40 % of 50 =

11 50 % of 40 % of 60 =   **15** 30 % of 40 % of 150 =

12 60 % of 50 % of 40 =   **16** 20 % of 30 % of $33\frac{1}{3}$ =

13 50 % of 40 % of 30 =   **17** 20 % of 30 % of 40 % of 250 =

18 I bought a cat and a dog, and then sold them for £ 60 each.
I made a 20 % profit on the sale of the dog and a 20 % loss on
the sale of the cat.
How much money did I make or lose?

T
A
S
T
E
R

T15 Skittles *A*   NC

oblem 0

) Joshua rolls one large ball at four skittles – numbered 1, 2, 3, 4.
His total score is the sum of the numbers on the skittles
knocked down.

  a How many ways are there to knock down just *one* skittle?
    And how many different totals can he get if just *one* skittle
    falls down?

  b How many ways are there to knock down just *two* skittles?
    And how many different totals can he get if just *two* skittles
    fall down?

he answer to question 0a is obvious. The four skittles all have different
ilues, so there are ___ ways to knock down just one skittle.
nd each way gives a different score, so there are ___ different scores.

uestion 0b is harder. You have to *be sure* that you don't miss any
issibilities – so you need a reliable *method* that lists them *all*.

ou could base your list of all possibilities on the *largest single*
ore – that is, the largest of the two numbers on the skittles
locked down.

  List all ways to knock down two skittles if the
  largest single score = 4

  then all ways if the *largest single score* = 3

  then all ways if the *largest single score* = 2.

he list will then be complete, because if two skittles are knocked down,
ie largest single score has to be *at least* 2.

  a **i**   How many different ways are there to knock down exactly
        four skittles?

      ii How many different total scores are there if all *four* skittles
         are knocked down?

  b **i**   How many different ways are there to knock down exactly
        zero skittles?

      ii How many different total scores are there if *zero* skittles are
         knocked down?

c When I *knock down* 4 skittles, I *leave* 0 skittles standing.
When I *knock down* 0 skittles, I *leave* 4 skittles standing.
That is, the number of ways to choose 4 skittles to *knock down* is equal to the number of ways to choose 4 skittles to *leave standing*.
How does this explain why the answers to parts **a** and **b** have to be equal?

2 **a** **i** How many different ways are there to knock down exactly *one* skittle?

   ii How many different total scores are there if just *one* skittle is knocked down?

  b **i** How many different ways are there to knock down exactly *three* skittles?

   ii How many different total scores are there if *three* skittles are knocked down?

  c When I *knock down* 3 skittles, I *leave* ___ skittle standing.
When I *knock down* 1 skittle, I *leave* ___ skittles standing.
That is, the number of ways to choose 3 skittles to *knock down* is equal to the number of ways to choose 3 skittles to *leave standing*!
How does this explain why the answers to **a** and **b** have to be equal?

3 **a** How many different ways are there to knock down exactly *two* skittles?

  b How many different total scores are there if exactly two skittles are knocked down?

4 Make a table collecting the answers to problems **1–3**.

Number of skittles knocked down	0	1	2	3	4
Number of different ways to do this	1				
Number of different total scores	1				

5 Suppose Joshua had five skittles to aim at, numbered 1, 2, 3, 4, 5.
Make a table like the table in problem 4.
Work out each entry carefully (and check them afterwards).

Number of skittles knocked down	0	1	2	3	4	5
Number of different ways to do this	1					
Number of different total scores	1					

T16 Cunning calculation *B*   NC

TASTER (vertical, right margin)

Problem 0

0 Calculate the answers *in your head* as efficiently as you can.

  a $(1234 \div 6) \times 12$ =

  b $(25 \div 6) \times 78$ =

  c $((123 \div 4) \times 56) \div 7$ =

Doing the calculation in problem **0a** in your head depends on noticing that 'divide by 6 and then multiply by 12' is the same as 'multiply by ___'. Use similar simplifications (while keeping your wits about you) to complete these as quickly as you can – with no mistakes.

1
  a $(12 \times 5) \div 5$ =
  b $(13 \times 10) \div 5$ =
  c $(14 \times 5) \div 10$ =
  d $(1234 \times 5) \div 10$ =

2
  a $(15 \div 5) \times 5$ =
  b $(20 \div 5) \times 10$ =
  c $(23 \div 10) \times 5$ =
  d $(123 \div 15) \times 5$ =

3
  a $(12 \times 17) \div 17$ =
  b $(13 \times 34) \div 17$ =
  c $(123 \times 17) \div 51$ =
  d $(1234 \times 17) \div 34$ =

4
  a $(12 \div 16) \times 16$ =
  b $(13 \div 16) \times 32$ =
  c $(123 \div 16) \times 16$ =
  d $(123 \div 48) \times 16$ =

5
  a $(12 \times 18) \div 6$ =
  b $(13 \times 34) \div 17$ =
  c $(14 \times 17) \div 34$ =
  d $(1234 \times 34) \div 68$ =

6
  a $(12 \div 16) \times 8$ =
  b $(13 \div 16) \times 8$ =
  c $(14 \div 16) \times 8$ =
  d $(1234 \div 16) \times 8$ =

7
  a $(4 \times 12) \div 4$ =
  b $(5 \times 12) \div 5$ =
  c $(6 \times 12) \div 6$ =
  d $(7 \times 12) \div 14$ =
  e $(8 \times 12) \div 24$ =
  f $(9 \times 12) \div 36$ =

8
  a $(12 \div 2) \times 4$ =
  b $(13 \div 3) \times 6$ =
  c $(14 \div 4) \times 8$ =
  d $(1234 \div 6) \times 12$ =

9
  a $(12 \times 5) \div 5$ =
  b $(12 \times 7) \div 14$ =
  c $(12 \times 9) \div 27$ =
  d $(1234 \times 11) \div 22$ =

  a $(91 \div 26) \times 14$ =   **b** $(234 \times 37) \div 222$ =

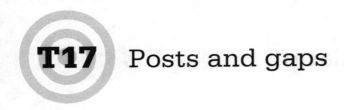

T17 Posts and gaps

Problem 0

> **0** How many three-digit integers are there?

Problem **0** highlights the fact that, when asked to count labelled objects with some specified beginning and end, there is often a danger of grabbing at an answer that is *one out*.

All the problems in this section are easy, but they are also easy to get wrong!

1 I start counting at 19 and go on to 89, taking one second to say each number.
How long do I take altogether?

2 Which number is halfway between 179 and 837?

3 **a** How many tears (along the perforations) must I make to reduce a strip of 12 postage stamps to single stamps?

    b How many tears (along the perforations) must I make to reduce a 12 by 12 sheet of postage stamps to single stamps?

4 I am going to fence off the end of my garden by first erecting wooden fence posts and then screwing 3 m wide panels to the fence posts. The garden is 36 m wide.
How many panels and how many fence posts must I order?

5 Twelve seedlings are planted in a row with equal spacing between neighbouring plants.
If the distance from the first seedling to the fourth is 12 cm, find the distance from the first to the ninth.

6 Each Saturday night I sell raffle tickets in my local pub. Last week the first ticket I sold was numbered 3748 and the last ticket I sold was numbered 3953.
How many tickets did I sell that night?

7 Ten bus stops are equally spaced along a bus route. The distance from the first to the third is 600 m.
How far is it from the first to the last?

8 I use drawing pins to pin up 10 photos (all the same size) in a row, with one drawing pin at each corner of each photo. Neighbouring photos share two drawing pins.

How many drawing pins do I use altogether?

9 In 2010 Christmas Day falls on a Saturday.

   a On what day does Christmas Day fall in 2009?

   b On what day does Christmas Day fall in 2011?

   c On what day does Christmas Day fall in 2008?

   d On what day does Christmas Day fall in 2012?

10 Five volumes of an encyclopedia, each volume 4 cm thick, are on a bookshelf in order from left to right: Vol. 1, Vol. 2, Vol. 3, Vol. 4, Vol. 5. A bookworm starts outside the front cover of Volume 1 and eats his way steadily (by the shortest route) through to the back cover of Volume 4.

How far does the bookworm travel?

T18 Think straight

This section is a mixture of logical puzzles and word problems that can be solved by a suitable calculation. But they all require you to think clearly.

Problem 0

> **0** 'All cats are animals, have whiskers and purr.'
> Which of the statements below *follows logically from these given facts*?
>
> **A** Any animal that purrs is a cat.
>
> **B** Some cats don't purr.
>
> **C** Some cats have whiskers.
>
> **D** Any animal with whiskers also purrs.
>
> **E** An animal with whiskers is always a cat.

1 Harold is 8 cm taller than Jack. Jim is 12 cm shorter than Harold. Jack is 125 cm tall. How tall is Jim?

2 Bilbo and Frodo have just consumed a plateful of cherries. Each repeats the rhyme 'Tinker, tailor, soldier, sailor, rich man, poor man, beggar man, thief' over and over again as he runs through his own heap of cherry stones. Bilbo finishes on 'sailor' whereas Frodo finishes on 'poor man'. What would they have finished on if they had run through both heaps together?

3 Jo is older than Ned. Kay is older than Olly, but younger than Ned. Mo is younger than Jo, but older than Olly. Pat is younger than Jo. Kay is older than Mo. Ned is younger than Pat. Order the six friends according to their ages – youngest first.

4 Ahmed, Brian, Chloe, Danielle, Ethel, Francis and George are choosing a team leader from among themselves. They stand in a circle, in alphabetical order, and count round (in the same order) rejecting every third person they come to; that person then leaves the circle. The last one left is to be team leader. If Ahmed is eventually elected, where must the counting have started?

5 Andrea, Brian and Clare spent an afternoon picking strawberries. Andrea picked 3 kg more than Brian but 2 kg less than Claire. If Brian picked three-quarters of the amount that Claire picked, what total weight did the three friends pick between them?

6 When Ann stands on Ben's shoulders she can just see over the wall. When Ben stands on Con's shoulders he can see nothing but bricks. When Con stands on Den's shoulders she can see over easily. Can you tell who are the tallest and the shortest?

7 Here are some facts about Mo's exam script.

  a No solution to a geometrical problem was marked wrong.

  b No tidy solution was written in green ink.

  c No erroneous solution scored any marks.

  d All Mo's solutions were written in green ink.

  e No untidy solution was free of errors.

Which of the following statements follow logically from these given facts?

  A Mo scored either zero or full marks on each question.

  B Mo answered no geometry questions.

  C Mo could not possibly have scored a lower mark.

  D Mo got at least one question right.

  E Every one of Mo's solutions was tidy.

8 Sue runs faster than Tariq, and Val always beats Uma. Wes is slower than Tariq. If all five race against each other, how many possible outcomes are there?

9 'If it rains, you'll get wet. If you get wet, you'll be sorry. If you're not sorry, I'll be cross.'
Which of the following statements can be deduced from these given facts?

  A You'll be cross.

  B I'll be sorry if you're cross.

  C I'll be sorry if it rains.

  D You'll be cross if I get wet.

0 Three boys (Vic, Wes, Zaheer) and two girls (Xi, Yvette) sit round a table. They come from five different towns – Ashton, Bacup, Cromer, Derby and Esher. The child from Ashton sits between Zaheer and the child from Esher. Neither of the girls sits next to Wes. Vic sits between Yvette and the child from Derby. Zaheer and the child from Cromer support different football teams.
Find the order round the table and where each child comes from.

T19 Order! Order! NC

The place value system means that integers are easy to recognise and to understand. However, other numbers are sometimes disguised. The most obvious way this happens is with fractions and decimals; different-looking fractions may be equal, and it is often not clear whether a given decimal is larger or smaller than a given fraction.

Problem 0

0 Write each set of numbers *in order, smallest first*. Put the appropriate symbol '<' or '=' between successive numbers in your final list.

a $\frac{3}{15}$ 0.315 $\frac{1}{5}$ **b** $\frac{3}{18}$ 0.16 $\frac{1}{6}$ 0.318

You could reach for a calculator. But you also need a method of your own. Part **a** illustrates what you have to look out for:

$$\frac{1}{5} = \frac{2}{10} = 0.2 \quad \text{and} \quad 0.2 < 0.315 \quad \therefore \quad \frac{1}{5} < 0.315.$$

Also $\quad \frac{1}{5} = \frac{2}{10} = \frac{3}{15} \quad \therefore \quad \frac{3}{15} = \frac{1}{5} < 0.315.$

Write out each set of numbers *in increasing order, smallest first* – inserting '<', '=' between successive terms in your list as appropriate.

1 $\frac{6}{9}$ 0.69 $\frac{3}{6}$ 0.36 **6** 0.375 $\frac{3}{8}$ 0.38 $\frac{19}{50}$

2 $\frac{3}{12}$ 0.312 $\frac{1}{4}$ 0.14 **7** 0.04 $\frac{1}{25}$ 0.125 $\frac{1}{8}$

3 $\frac{3}{4}$ 0.34 $\frac{21}{28}$ 0.2128 **8** 1.125 $\frac{9}{8}$ 0.98 $\frac{49}{50}$

4 $\frac{1}{2}$ 0.12 $\frac{5}{10}$ 0.510 **9** $\frac{3}{75}$ 0.375 $\frac{3}{8}$ 0.04

5 $\frac{5}{4}$ 0.54 1.25 $\frac{27}{50}$

10 $\frac{3}{25}$ 0.12 $\frac{13}{40}$ 0.325

11 2.25 $\frac{9}{4}$ 0.94 $\frac{27}{12}$ $\frac{47}{50}$

12 $\frac{2}{7}$ 0.27 $\frac{6}{21}$ 0.621

T20 Multiplication: Decimals A NC

Decimal multiplication arises naturally in calculations involving measures.

Problem 0

> **0** Cloth is sold in fixed *widths*. The price is given in '£ per metre *length*'.
>
>   **a** What should you pay for 2 m of cloth priced at £9 per metre?
>
>   **b** What should you pay for 17.3 m of cloth priced at £9 per metre?

a If each metre costs £9, then 2 m would cost $2 \times £9 = £\underline{}$.

b 17 m of cloth would cost $\underline{} \times £9 = £\underline{}$

0.3 m of cloth would cost $\frac{3}{10} \times £9 = £\underline{}$

∴ 17.3 m would cost $£\underline{} + £\underline{} = £\underline{}$.

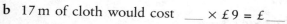

To calculate this directly (without working out 17×9 and 0.3×9 separately), we note that 17.3 m of cloth costs
$$17 \times £9 + 0.3 \times £9 = (17 + 0.3) \times £9 = £(17.3 \times 9).$$
So we have to calculate 17.3×9.

$$17.3 \times 9 = (173 \div 10) \times 9 = \frac{1}{10}(173 \times 9)$$

$$= 155.7$$

```
    1 7 3
  ×     9
  ─────────
  1 5 5 7
```

∴ A 17.3 m length of cloth priced at £9 per metre would cost £155.70.

If the cloth was priced at £9.40 per metre we would have to calculate

$$17.3 \times 9.4 = (173 \div 10) \times (94 \div 10)$$

$$= \left(\tfrac{1}{10} \times 173\right) \times \left(\tfrac{1}{10} \times 94\right) = \frac{1}{100}\left(173 \times 94\right)$$

$$= 162.62$$

```
    1 7 3
  ×   9 4
  ─────────
      6 9 2
  1 5 5 7 0
  ─────────
  1 6 2 6 2
```

∴ A 17.3 m length of cloth priced at £9.40 per metre would cost £162.62.

Use decimal multiplication to calculate these.
(Check your working for the first few by repeating the calculation in
your head.)

1	7.5×4	=		10	2.5×17	=
2	2.5×7	=		11	2.4×26	=
3	2.4×6	=		12	3.5×38	=
4	3.5×8	=		13	3.8×49	=
5	3.8×9	=		14	6.3×58	=
6	6.3×8	=		15	9.2×67	=
7	9.2×7	=		16	7.6×75	=
8	7.6×5	=		17	27.4×8.9	=
9	7.5×14	=		18	43.8×7.3	=

19 $287.4 \times 8.9 =$ 20 $453.8 \times 47.3 =$

Weights are usually given in *tonnes*, *kilograms* or *grams*; so you have to be able to switch between grams and kilograms, and between kilograms and tonnes. In the same way, you have to be completely at home with *kilometres*, *metres*, *centimetres* and *millimetres*, and with other standard measures, and be able to change confidently *from one unit to another*.

When you do calculations (to work out costs, or speeds, or distance travelled), then with decimal measures like these it makes sense to use decimal arithmetic – so *each quantity has to be expressed as a decimal*.

Problem 0

0 **a** How many *centimetres* are there in 16 km 37 m 8 cm?

16 km 37 m 8 cm = ___ cm

  b How many *kilometres* are there in 16 km 37 m 8 cm?

16 km 37 m 8 cm = ___ km

1 Which of the following quantities are equal to each other?

3 kg $\frac{3}{10000}$ km

0.3 m   30 cl

3 g $\frac{3}{100}$ litre

30 mm   0.003 kg

30 kg   30 ml

$\frac{3}{10}$ litre   0.03 tonne

$\frac{3}{1000}$ tonne   0.03 m

2 How many minutes are there in $2\frac{1}{3}$ hours?

3 Express 750 g as a percentage of 2 kg.

4 Which is greater?

    a 4.5 m or 45 cm?   **d** 1000 s or 20 min?

    b 91 kg or 910 g?   **e** £ 16.20 or 162 p?

    c 1230 cm or 1.23 m?   **f** 120 kg or 1.2 tonnes?

5 How many 60 cm pieces of string can I cut from a piece of string 8m 40 cm long?

6 Express each quantity in terms of the specified units (using decimals where necessary).

    a 2 m 12 cm = ___ cm   **i** 9 km 81 m = ___ km

    b 2 h 20 min = ___ min   **j** 796 cl = ___ litres

    c 28 kg 30 g = ___ g   **k** 27 cm 4 mm = ___ m

    d 3 m 33 cm = ___ m   **l** 7 cm = ___ m

    e 4 h 15 min = ___ h   **m** 2 m 2 cm = ___ m

    f 7 m 7 mm = ___ m   **n** 23 kg 17 g = ___ kg

    g 44999 p = £ ___   **o** 23 m 76 cm = ___ km

    h 3 m 4 mm = ___ m

7 **a** How should you write the number 'eleven thousand, eleven hundred and eleven'?

    b How should you write 'ninety-nine thousand, ninety-nine hundred and ninety-nine'?

Where did the money go? *A*

Calculating is relatively straightforward: the recipe and the ingredients are given; you only have to combine them correctly to get the answer.

Solving problems is often more like detective work: you are given the outcome, and must then work out how it was obtained.

Problem 0

0 a Five people share a prize of £17.55.
How much should each person receive?

b I bought some Swizzles and some Stickies for 48p. Swizzles cost 5p each; Stickies cost 6p each.
How many of each did I buy?

1 Swizzles cost 9p each.
If I buy seven Swizzles, how much change will I get from £1?

2 Two girls earn £60 between them. Rose earns £3 for every £2 that Jo earns.
How much does Jo earn?

3 I spent £25 on some fish. Each goldfish cost £5; each angel fish cost £3.
How many of each did I buy?

4 In a small cafe the average pay of the five workers is £120 per week.
If the four waiters get an average of £100 per week, how much does the cook get?

5 Andy has twice as much money as Brigitte, and Carl has half as much again as Andy. Carl has 20p less than Di, who has £2.
How much has Andy?

6 My Christmas present cost £1 plus half its price.
What did it cost?

7 a Three friends earned £200 cutting lawns. They reckoned that John and Mark did three times as much work between them as Ben, and that Mark did twice as much as John.
How much of the money should go to John?

b On another occasion they earned £180 by cutting lawns. This time John did half as much as Ben and Mark combined, and Ben did twice as much as Mark.
How much of the money should go to Ben?

8 a What is the largest amount of money less than £1 that I can have in standard British coins without being able to pay exactly 50p?

b What is the largest amount of money that I can have in standard British coins *excluding £2 coins* without being able to pay exactly £1?

9 I spent exactly £10 on some fish. Each goldfish cost £0.90; each angel fish cost £0.70.
How many of each type did I buy?

10 I spent £3 on some eggs direct from a friendly farmer. Extra large eggs cost 50p each; medium-sized eggs cost 20p each; small eggs cost 10p each. For two of these sizes I bought the same number of eggs.
How many of each size did I buy?
How many different solutions are there?

T23 Buy one, get one free *B*   NC

Once you know **12 × 3 = 36** you should be able to work out lots of other multiplications in your head. For example,

$$12 \times 3 = 36 \text{ is just another way of saying } 36 \div 3 = 12;$$

and

$$120 \times 3 = (10 \times 12) \times 3$$
$$= 10 \times (12 \times 3)$$
$$= 10 \times 36 = 360.$$

Problem 0

0 Have a go at these *without working them out the long way.*

a 36 ÷ 12 =	**e** 3600 ÷ 30 =
b 12 × 30 =	**f** 1.2 × 3 =
c 360 ÷ 3 =	**g** 360 ÷ 12 =
d 120 × 30 =	**h** 1.2 × 30 =

1 Work out the answer to 1088 × 3 =

Use the answer to problem **1** to answer problem **2** by 'thinking' (not by calculating).

2 a 1088 × 30	=	**h** 3264 ÷ 30 =	
b 10880 × 3	=	**i** 1088 × 0.3 =	
c 108.8 × 3	=	**j** 0.1088 × 3 =	
d 3264 ÷ 3	=	**k** 32.64 ÷ 0.3 =	
e 32640 ÷ 3	=	**l** 1.088 × 0.3 =	
f 1088 × 300	=	**m** 0.3264 ÷ 0.03 =	
g 3.264 ÷ 1.088 =			

3 a Work out 823 × 15.
Use this to write down the answer to 0.12345 ÷ 0.015.

b Work out 1286 × 96.
Use this to write down the answer to 0.0123456 ÷ 12.86.

T24 Calculation with measures A

The simplest application of arithmetic is in problems involving measures.

Problem 0

0 A snail crawls 30 cm in 30 seconds.

  a At this pace, how far would the snail crawl in 1 hour?

  b At the same pace, how far would the snail crawl in 1 day?

  c At the same pace, roughly how long would the snail take to crawl 1 km?

1 A motorbike travels at 20 m per second.

  a How far will the motorbike travel in 1 minute?

  b What is the motorbike's speed in km/h?

  c How long will the motorbike take to travel 1 km?

2 18 litres of orange juice are poured into 50 cl glasses. How many glasses can be filled?

3 A cyclist travels at 25 m per second.

  a Calculate the distance travelled in 4 seconds.

  b How long will the cyclist take to cover 1 km?

  c Calculate the cyclist's speed in km/h.

4 How many 60 cm lengths of wood can be cut from a wooden plank 8 m 40 cm long?

5 Two cyclists cycle towards each other along a road. At 8 am they are 42 km apart. At 11 am they meet. One cyclist pedals at an average speed of 7.5 km/h.
What is the average speed of the other cyclist?

6 A car travels 3 km in 2.5 min.

   a Find the speed of the car in km/h.

   b How long does it take to travel 1 km?

7 A horse covers 2.4 km in 5 minutes.

   a What is the horse's speed in km/h?

   b How long does the horse take to run 1 km?

8 A baker uses 6 kg of flour to make 60 large rolls.

   a How many rolls can he make with 2.4 kg of flour?

   b How much flour does he need to make 25 rolls?

T25 Missing digits *A*

Problem 0

0 Work out the missing digits in this sum	$\begin{array}{r} 6\ 7 \\ +\ \square\ 6 \\ \hline \square\ 5\ \square \end{array}$

Work out the missing digits in each of these sums. (The 'leading' digit is never a 0.)

1
$$\begin{array}{r} 8\ \square \\ +\ \square\ 4 \\ \hline \square\ 7 \end{array}$$

5
$$\begin{array}{r} \square\ 3\ 8 \\ +\ \ \ \ 6\ \square \\ \hline \square\ 0\ \square\ 0 \end{array}$$

2
$$\begin{array}{r} \square\ 7 \\ +\ 7\ \square \\ \hline \square\ 3 \end{array}$$

6
$$\begin{array}{r} 3\ \square\ 4 \\ -\ \square\ 2\ \square \\ \hline 1\ 8\ 6 \end{array}$$

3
$$\begin{array}{r} 3\ \square \\ +\ \ \square\ 8 \\ \hline \square\ 1\ 1 \end{array}$$

7
$$\begin{array}{r} 4\ 8\ \square \\ -\ \square\ 6\ 8 \\ \hline \square\ 3 \end{array}$$

4
$$\begin{array}{r} \square\ 2 \\ +\ \ 8\ \square \\ \hline \square\ 0\ 1 \end{array}$$

8 Fit the digits 1, 2, 3, 4, 5, 6, 7, 8 into the eight spaces to make this subtraction correct.

$$\begin{array}{r} \square\ \square\ \square \\ -\ \square\ \square\ \square \\ \hline \square\ \square \end{array}$$

Word problems A NC

rithmetic too often gets stuck in a world of numbers and numerals.
requires effort to make elementary arithmetic part of the way we
ink about the *real* world. Word problems are not always real, but they
elp develop the skills needed to link the world of mathematics to
e real world.

oblem 0

At the school fair, Albert, Bertha and Charlie all tried to guess
the number of *Smarties* in a jar. Albert guessed 131, Bertha
guessed 123 and Charlie guessed 129. They were all wrong,
but one was close, while the other two missed the true number
by the same amount.
How many *Smarties* were there in the jar?

The average height of two boys is 1.65 m.
If one boy is 0.02 m taller than the other boy, find the height of the
shorter boy.

In an enclosure there are 14 animals – a mixture of geese and
rabbits. These animals have 40 feet between them.
How many geese are there?
How many rabbits are there?

Which provides the larger shares: two bars of chocolate shared
fairly between three people, or five bars shared between seven
people?

A hotel buys four identical televisions and two identical radios
for £756.
If each television costs £180, what is the price of a radio?

Ian started to walk from A to B, but gave up 6 miles after he had
passed the halfway mark. He was then 5 miles from B.
How far is it from A to B?

6 Snow White wants to weigh Bashful, Dopey and Sleepy. They refuse to be weighed separately, but agree to be weighed in pairs. Bashful and Dopey weigh in at 17 stone; Dopey and Sleepy weigh in at 15 stone; Sleepy and Bashful weigh in at 20 stone. How much does each Dwarf weigh?

7 My glass is half-full. When I add 50 ml, the glass is two-thirds full. How much liquid does my glass hold when full?

8 Anna put some 2 p coins on the table – half 'heads up' and half 'tails up'. Anna then chose three of the coins and turned them over, after which two-thirds of the coins were 'heads up'. How many coins were on the table? How many different solutions are there?

9 The houses in a street are to be numbered from 1 to 140 using new brass numerals. How many 2s are needed?

10 A milk bottle weighs 410 g when one-quarter full, and 460 g when one-third full.

   a What does the bottle itself weigh when empty?

   b What does the bottle weigh when half-full?

11 Two years ago the ages of the Seven Dwarfs totalled 30 years. What will their total age be in three years' time?

12 The Queen of Hearts baked some tarts. Next day in the market her maid sold $\frac{3}{5}$ of the tarts in the morning, and $\frac{1}{4}$ of the remainder in the afternoon. If she sold 200 more tarts in the morning than in the afternoon, how many tarts did the Queen of Hearts bake?

13 The floor of a square hall is tiled with identical square tiles. Along the two diagonals there are 89 tiles altogether. What is the total number of tiles on the floor?

14 Anna put some 2 p coins on the table – half 'heads up' and half 'tails up'. Anna then chose five of the coins and turned them over, after which two-thirds of the coins were 'heads up'. How many coins were on the table?

CORE

Whenever you need to use pencil and paper for multiplication, long
multiplication is likely to be the most efficient and reliable method.
So you must learn to do long multiplication quickly and accurately.

But you should also be alert to the possibility of short cuts – especially

a when 'trading' factors makes the calculation easier:

for example $15 \times 26 = 15 \times (2 \times 13)$
$\qquad\qquad\quad = (15 \times 2) \times 13$
$\qquad\qquad\quad = 30 \times 13$
$\qquad\qquad\quad = \underline{\quad}$

$\qquad 50 \times 14 = 50 \times (2 \times 7)$
$\qquad\qquad\quad = (50 \times 2) \times 7$
$\qquad\qquad\quad = \underline{\quad}$

or where it is possible to combine 2s and 5s to make 10 or 100:

for example $8 \times 75 = (2 \times 4) \times (25 \times 3)$
$\qquad\qquad\quad = 2 \times (4 \times 25) \times 3$
$\qquad\qquad\quad = \underline{\quad}$

$\qquad 14 \times 15 = (7 \times 2) \times (5 \times 3)$
$\qquad\qquad\quad = 7 \times (2 \times 5) \times 3$
$\qquad\qquad\quad = \underline{\quad}$

b when multiplying by '1 less' or by '1 more' than an easy multiplier:

for example $39 \times 30 = (40 - 1) \times 30$
$\qquad\qquad\quad = 40 \times 30 - 1 \times 30$
$\qquad\qquad\quad = 1200 - 30$
$\qquad\qquad\quad = \underline{\quad}$

roblem 0

0 $15 \times 75 \times 40 =$

1 $25 \times 12 =$ | **7** $99 \times 83 =$
2 $19 \times 13 =$ | **8** $35 \times 26 =$
3 $18 \times 15 =$ | **9** $22 \times 49 =$
4 $22 \times 15 =$ | **10** $35 \times 202 =$
5 $28 \times 75 =$ | **11** $222 \times 15 =$
6 $19 \times 15 =$

2 $125 \times 35 \times 52 \times 40 =$

C2 What's my number? A NC

These problems are not hard. But you should solve them by calculating, *not by guessing.* There may be more than one answer – so keep alert, and make sure that you do not miss any possibilities.

Problem 0

> **0** I am thinking of a number between 10 and 20. When divided by 3, the remainder is 2.
>
> **a** The sum of the digits is odd.
>   What is my number?
>
> **b** Suppose the sum of the digits is even.
>   What can you tell me about my number?

1 A number is a factor of 72. It is also a multiple of 8. It lies between 10 and 50. What is the number?

2 I am thinking of a number between 10 and 20. The sum of its digits is a prime number, and the original number is an exact multiple of this prime number. What is my number?

3 $\frac{3}{8}$ of a number is 27.

What is $\frac{1}{2}$ of the number?

4 I am thinking of a number less than 50. It is a multiple of 7 and its digits differ by 1. What is my number?

5 I am thinking of a number less than 30. When divided by 7 the remainder is 3. When divided by 5 the remainder is 2. What is my number?

6 I am thinking of a number less than 50. My number is a multiple of 7 and its digits add to 10. What is my number?

7 I am thinking of a number less than 100. Its digits add to 10. When I divide my number by 9 the remainder is 1. What can you tell me about my number?

8 I am thinking of a number less than 50. When divided by 6 the remainder is 2; when divided by 5 the remainder is 4. The sum of the digits is even. What is my number?

9 I am thinking of a number between 20 and 100. The sum of the digits is divisible by 8, and when my number is divided by 8 the remainder is 1. What is my number?

10 If I gave everyone 2 apples, there would be 2 left over.
If I tried to give everyone 4 apples, I would have 4 too few.
How many apples are there and how many people?

11 a How many of the integers from 11 to 30 are divisible by the sum of their digits?

   b How many of the integers from 31 to 50 are divisible by the sum of their digits?

   c How many of the integers from 51 to 70 are divisible by the sum of their digits?

   d How many of the integers from 71 to 90 are divisible by the sum of their digits?

   e How many of the integers from 91 to 99 are divisible by the sum of their digits?

CORE

CORE

Sometimes integer multiplication can be done in clever ways. But unless the numbers are very special, multiplication is best done in column form – with units, tens and hundreds columns lined up.

For example, to calculate 73 × 649, write

First multiply the units: 3 × 649 = 1947
Then multiply the tens: 70 × 649 = 45430
making sure that you enter the digits of your answer in the correct column.
Finally, combine the two parts to get the *answer*.

```
        6 4 9
  ×       7 3
      1 9 4 7
    4 5 4 3 0
    4 7 3 7 7
```

Problem 0

0 Fill in the missing digits in the long multiplication.

```
                6 4 9
        ×         4 7
          4 □ 4 □
        □ 5 □ □ 0
        □ □ □ □ □
```

Work out these multiplications in the same way.
Do *not* use a calculator.

1 91 × 11 =

2 77 × 13 =

3 823 × 15 =

4 97 × 56 =

5 953 × 57   =

6 9009 × 37   =

7 5439 × 143 =

8 15873 × 49 =

9 Work out the missing digits in these multiplications.

a
```
        □ □ □
  ×       □ 3
      □ 2 4 7
    □ □ □ 4 □
    □ □ □ □ □
```

b
```
          □ 7
  ×       □ □
      4 □ □
    □ □ 6 □
    □ □ □ 5
```

Analogue angles

Make sure you can see a clockface before tackling this task.

◎ What is the angle between the two hands of a clock

    ◎ at 6 o'clock?

    ◎ at 3 o'clock?

    ◎ at 12 o'clock?

Problem 0

0 a What is the angle between the two hands of a clock at 6:30?

  b Give another time when the angle between the hands is the same as at 6:30.

1 What angle does the minute hand of a clock turn through

  a in 1 hour?   **c** in $\frac{1}{2}$ hour?

  b in 3 hours?

2 What angle does the hour hand of a clock turn through

  a in 1 hour?   **c** in $\frac{1}{2}$ hour?

  b in 3 hours?

3 What angle does the minute hand of a clock turn through

  a in 15 minutes?   **c** in 50 minutes?

  b in 20 minutes?   **d** in 35 minutes?

4 What angle does the hour hand of a clock turn through

  a in 15 minutes?   **c** in 50 minutes?

  b in 20 minutes?   **d** in 35 minutes?

5 a What is the angle between the two hands of a clock at 3 pm?

  b Give another time (other than 3 am!) when the angle between the hands is the same as at 3 pm.

6   a   What is the angle between the two hands of a clock at 2 pm?

     b   Give another time when the angle between the hands is the same.

7   a   What is the angle between the two hands of a clock at 4 pm?

     b   Give another time when the angle between the hands is the same.

8   What angle does the *second* hand of a clock turn through in 5 minutes?

9   a   What is the angle between the two hands of a clock at 2:30 pm?

     b   Give another time when the angle between the hands is the same.

10   a   What is the angle between the two hands of a clock at 3:30 pm?

     b   Give another time when the angle between the hands is the same.

11   a   What is the angle between the two hands of a clock at 4:20 pm?

     b   Give another time when the angle between the hands is the same.

12   a   What is the angle between the two hands of a clock at 7:15 pm?

     b   Give another time when the angle between the hands is the same.

C5 Tables with remainders   NC

you know your tables, and think carefully what each equation is
ying, then you should be able to work out the numbers that go in the
xes to make these equations correct.

oblem 0

a ☐ ÷ 4 = 5 remainder 1

b This one is a wee bit harder.

'☐3' stands for a two-digit number with units digit '3'.

'☐3' ÷ 7 = ☐ remainder 1

This says that when you divide the (unknown) two-digit
number '☐3' by 7, you end up with a remainder of 1.

You have to work out *the unknown tens digit*, and *how
many times* 7 goes into the two-digit number '☐3'!

w try these.

☐ ÷ 5   = 3 remainder 1   **7** '3☐' ÷ 8   = ☐ remainder 6

☐ ÷ 6   = 9 remainder 4   **8** '☐3' ÷ 7   = ☐ remainder 1

45 ÷ ☐   = 7 remainder 3   **9** '6☐' ÷ 7   = ☐ remainder 5

56 ÷ ☐   = 6 remainder 2   **10** '☐3' ÷ ☐ = 12 remainder 5

'7☐' ÷ ☐ = 12 remainder 7   **11** '5☐' ÷ 13   = ☐ remainder 7

63 ÷ ☐   = 7 remainder 7

How many different solutions are there to these calculations?

a '☐5' + ☐ = 8 remainder 7

b '☐3' + ☐ = 8 remainder 5

C6 Counting the ways *B*

CORE

Calculating is a bit like cooking a simple meal: the ingredients and recipe are given; you only have to combine them correctly and follow the recipe.

Mathematics is more than calculation: you need to be able to calculate quickly and accurately so that you can work backwards like a detective, that is,

> you are given some outcome (or a meal already prepared),
> and you have to work how it arose (or what went into it).

Problem 0

---

0 Three monkeys eat a total of 17 nuts.

    a Calculate the average number of nuts eaten by each of the three monkeys.
What does this tell you about the *smallest* number of nuts eaten by any of the three monkeys?

    b **i** Suppose that the number of nuts eaten by each monkey is an odd number bigger than 1, and that no two monkeys eat the same number of nuts.
How many nuts does each of the three monkeys eat?
How many different solutions are there?

       ii Suppose that all you know is that each monkey eats an odd number of nuts.
How many different solutions would there be then?

To find all possible solutions without missing any, there is little point just trying numbers to see if they work: you need a *method*.
Part **a** provides one way of organising your search.

Not everyone can be above average; so at least one monkey has to eat *fewer than* ___ nuts.
Now consider the possible *smallest* numbers in turn:

    in **bi**   there are just ___ possibilities for this smallest number;

    in **bii**   there are ___ possibilities for this smallest number.

1 Four birds laid 22 eggs between them. Each bird laid an odd number of eggs.
If no two birds laid the same number of eggs, how many eggs did each bird lay?
How many different solutions are there?

2 Tripods have three legs; Bipods have two legs. There are at least two of each and there are 23 legs altogether.
How many Tripods are there?
How many Bipods?

3 In a fairground shooting gallery each target has a different score which is a positive integer. My three shots hit different targets, each score is an odd number and my total is 19.
What can you tell about my three scores?
How many different solutions are there?

4 Three monkeys ate a total of 25 nuts. Each monkey ate an odd number of nuts and the three odd numbers were all different and bigger than 1.
How many different solutions are there?

5 When playing mini-cricket in the back garden a *boundary* scores either 5 or 7. I hate running, so I try to score all my runs in boundaries, with at least one boundary of each kind.
What is the smallest score that can be achieved like this in two different ways?

C7   Drawing conclusions *B*

The aim of this section is for you to *think about the mathematics behind the constructions*. There are two separate parts to any construction:

    i   the procedure being followed

    ii   the way you implement that procedure.

Because eyes, fingers and pencils are imperfect, part **ii** is inevitably *approximate*; this is neither surprising nor mathematically interesting. What matters mathematically is whether part **i** – that is, *the procedure being followed* – is **exact in principle**.

Problem 0

> **0**   Draw a line segment *OA* (roughly 5 cm long).
> Draw the circle *C* with centre *O* and passing through the point *A*.
>
> Draw the circle C_1 with centre *A* and passing through the point *O*. Let these two circles cross at *B* and *F*.
>
> **a**   Without measuring, what do you *know* about the line segments *OA* and *OF*? Explain your answer.
>
> **b**   Without measuring, what do you *know* about the line segments *AB* and *AF*? Explain your answer.
>
> **c**   So what do you *know* about the triangles *OAB* and *OAF*?
>
> **d**   And what does this tell you about the three angles $\angle ABO$? $\angle BOA$? $\angle OAB$? Explain your answer.

Problem **1** extends your construction from problem **0**.

1   In problem **0** you started with two points *O* and *A* and constructed two new points *B*, *F*. You should now build on this figure and construct additional points *C*, *D*, *E* as follows.

    a   Draw the circle C_2 with centre *B* and passing through the point *A*.
How do you know that this circle has to pass through the point *O*?
Let the circle C_2 cut the circle *C* at the points *A* and *C*.

      i   Without measuring, what do you *know* about the line segments *BA*, *BC*? Explain your answer.

      ii   What do you *know* about the triangle *OBC*?

b Draw the circle C_3 with centre C and passing through the point B.
How do you know that this circle has to pass through the point O?
Let the circle C_3 cut the circle C at the point (B and) D.

   i Without measuring, what do you *know* about the line segments CB, CD?
Explain your answer.

   ii What do you *know* about the triangle OCD?

c Draw the circle C_4 with centre D and passing through the point C.
How do you know that this circle has to pass through the point O?
Let the circle C_4 cut the circle C at the point (C and) E.

   i Without measuring, what do you *know* about the line segments DC, DE?
Explain your answer.

   ii What do you *know* about the triangle ODE?

d Draw the circle C_5 with centre E and passing through the point D.
How do you know that this circle has to pass through the point O?
How do you know that this circle has to pass through the point F?
What do you know about the hexagon $ABCDEF$? (You should explain why all six sides are equal and why all six angles are equal.)

2 a Draw a line segment AB of length $5\,\text{cm}$.

b Use a protractor to construct a point X such that $\angle BAX = 108°$, and a point Y on the same side of AB as X such that $\angle ABY = 108°$.
Draw the line AX and the line BY.

c Draw the circle with centre A through the point B; let this circle meet the line AX at the point E.
Draw the circle with centre B through the point A; let this circle meet the line BY at the point C.

d Draw the circle with centre E through the point A, and the circle with centre C through the point B.
These two circles meet at two points – a point D' near the segment AB, and a point D on the opposite side of the line EC.

e What do you expect to be true of the polygon $ABCDE$?
Can you be sure that the five sides are all equal?
What about the five angles?

3 a Draw a line segment *AB* of length 5 cm.

b Use a protractor to construct a point *X* such that ∠*BAX* = 108°, and a point *Y* on the same side of *AB* as *X* such that ∠*ABY* = 108°.
Draw the line *AX* and the line *BY*.

c Construct the bisector of ∠*BAX* and the bisector of ∠*ABY*. Let these bisectors meet at the point *O*. Without measuring, what do you *know* about *OA* and *OB*?
Explain your answer.

d Draw the circle *C* with centre *O* through the points *A* and *B*. Let this circle cut the line *AX* at the point *E* and the line *BY* at the point *C*.

  i Without measuring, say what you *know* about *OA* and *OE*.

  ii So what kind of triangle is △*OAE*?
  What does this guarantee about ∠*OEA*?
  So what do you know about ∠*AOE*?

  iii What does this tell you about △*OEA* and △*OAB*?
  So what do you know about the two segments *EA* and *AB*?

  iv Similarly, show that △*OBC* is congruent to △*OAB*.
  Conclude that *AB* = *BC*.

e Draw the circle with centre *C* through the point *B*. Let this circle meet the circle *C* again at the point *D*.

  i Explain why △*OCD* is congruent to △*OBC*.

  ii What does this imply about ∠*DOE*?
  Explain why *DE* = *AB*.

f Go back over the previous steps and explain why you can be sure that all five sides and all five angles of the pentagon *ABCDE* are equal.

Problem 0

0 Work out the missing digits in this sum.

```
      6 9
      □ 5
  +   7 □
  ─────────
    □ 4 3
```

Work out the missing digits in these sums. The *leading* digit is never a 0.

1
```
    2 □
    □ 4
  + 8 4
  ───────
  2 □ 2
```

3
```
    6 □ 7
    □ 6 8
  + 3 9 □
  ─────────
  2 □ 1 1
```

2
```
    9 □
    □ 4
  + 9 3
  ───────
  1 □ 9
```

4
```
    2 □ 7
    □ 1 5
  + □ 4 □
  ─────────
  2 □ 8 1
```

5 a
```
    □ 3 □
  - 3 □ 6
  ───────
    1 3 5
```

c
```
    3 □ 5 8
  - □ 7 7 □
  ─────────
    8 □ 9
```

b
```
    □ □ 4
  - 7 4 □
  ───────
      7 5
```

6 Fit the digits 1, 2, 3, 4, 5, 6 into this subtraction to make it correct.

How many different solutions are there?

```
    □ □ □
  - □ □ □
  ───────
      7 8
```

C9 Division: Integers

There are three good reasons for working hard to master the standard algorithm for division.

◎ It develops the mental arithmetic learned in primary school.

◎ It is one of the simplest examples of the kind of multi-step procedures, or algorithms, which lie at the heart of modern mathematics.

◎ It is essential if you are later to understand decimals.

Each of these reasons is enough to make division a key objective.

Do these short divisions using the standard layout.

Problem 0

0 a $3\overline{)654}$

∴ **654 = 3** × ____

c $11\overline{)1001}$

∴ **1001 = 11** × ____

b $3\overline{)123}$

∴ **123 = 3** × ____

d $3\overline{)924}$

∴ **924 = 3** × ____

For example, to calculate 654 ÷ 3, write: $3\overline{)654}$

First divide 3 into **6** (or rather into 600) to get 600 = 200 × 3
    that is,   6 hundreds = (2 × 3) hundreds + 0 tens

Say '3 into 6 goes **2** times, with remainder **0**': write $3\overline{)6\,^05\,4}$ with **2** above

Next divide 3 into 05: 05 = 3 × 1 remainder 2: write $3\overline{)65\,^24}$ with **2 1** above

Next divide 3 into 24: 24 = 3 × 8 remainder 0: write $3\overline{)65\,^24}$ with **2 1 8** above

∴ 654 = 3 × **218**

Use short division to work out each of these divisions in the same way. Do **not** use a calculator.

1 4)5 4 3 2

∴ **5432 = 4 × __**

2 3)1 2 3 4 5

∴ **12 345 = 3 × __**

3 3)5 4 3 2 1

∴ **54 321 = 3 × __**

4 5)1 2 3 4 5

∴ **12 345 = 5 × __**

5 7)5 4 3 2

∴ **5432 = 7 × __**

6 11)1 2 3 1 2 3

∴ **123 123 = 11 × __**

7 7)1 1 1 9 3

∴ **11 193 = 7 × __**

8 13)1 5 9 9

∴ **1599 = 13 × __**

9 8)5 4 3 2

∴ **5432 = 8 × __**

10 13)2 0 0 2

∴ **2002 = 13 × __**

11 21)3 0 0 3

∴ **3003 = 21 × __**

12 37)3 3 3 3 3 3

∴ **333 333 = 37 × __**

13 49)7 7 7 7 7 7

∴ **777 777 = 49 × __**

14 Work out the missing digits in these divisions.

      1 5
a 7)1 ☐ ☐

            2 ☐
b 8)☐ 3 ☐

15 Replace the ☐ by the digits 1, 2, 3, 4, 5 (used once each) to make this division correct.

      ☐ ☐
    ☐)☐ ☐

C10 Tiling A

In a *tiling* you have to cover a large shape with copies of a given *tile* – in much the same way as bathroom walls are covered with small square tiles. The tiles must fit edge-to-edge *with no overlap*.

If the large shape can be completely covered, then the tiling is *complete*. Sometimes a complete tiling is impossible.

Problem 0

0 Suppose you have a large supply of 2 by 1 rectangles.

  a You want to tile a 2 by 2 square. How many 2 by 1 tiles do you need?

  b Suppose you want to tile a 3 by 3 square.
     i What is the largest number of 1 by 1 squares you could expect to cover with 2 by 1 tiles?
     ii How many 2 by 1 tiles do you need to cover the squares that can be covered?
     iii Show how to tile a 3 by 3 square leaving the minimum possible number of squares uncovered.

1 **a** Show how to tile a 4 by 4 square with 2 by 1 tiles.
  b Show how to tile a 6 by 6 square with 2 by 1 tiles.

2 When you 'almost tile' a 3 by 3 square with 2 by 1 tiles, how many possible locations are there for the empty square(s)?

3 Suppose you want to tile a 5 by 5 square.
  a What is the smallest possible number of squares that remain uncovered?
  b How many 2 by 1 tiles do you need for this 'almost tiling'?
  c Show how to tile a 5 by 5 square leaving the minimum possible number of squares uncovered.
  d When you 'almost tile' a 5 by 5 square with 2 by 1 tiles, how many possible locations are there for the empty square(s)?

CORE

4 Suppose you want to tile a 7 by 7 square.

   a What is the smallest possible number of squares that remain uncovered?

   b How many 2 by 1 tiles do you need for this 'almost tiling'?

   c Show how to tile a 7 by 7 square leaving the minimum possible number of squares uncovered.

   d When you 'almost tile' a 7 by 7 square with 2 by 1 tiles, how many possible locations are there for the empty square(s)?

5 a For which values of n is it possible to tile an n by n square completely with 2 by 1 tiles?
(In question **0a** you showed how to tile a 2 by 2 square.
How could you use this to *prove* that an n by n square can always be tiled for all the larger values you have specified?)

   b In questions 2 and 3 you showed that when $n = 3$ or $n = 5$ it is possible to 'almost tile' an n by n square with 2 by 1 tiles – leaving just ___ square uncovered.
How would you *prove* that the same is true for *all* values of n not covered by part **a**?

C11 Highest common factors and least common multiples *A*

NC

◎ 2 is a factor of both 12 and 18; it is a *common factor* of 12 and 18.
12 and 18 have four *common factors* – namely 1, 2, 3 and 6.

6 is the *largest*, or highest, of these common factors of 12 and 18: it is called the **highest common factor** (or **hcf**) of 12 and 18:

$$hcf(12, 18) = 6.$$

◎ 24 is a multiple of 12, but not of 18;
36 is a multiple of 18 and a multiple of 12, so 36 is a *common multiple* of 18 and of 12.

72 is also a *common multiple* of 18 and of 12; but it is bigger than 36.
36 is the smallest, or **least common multiple (lcm)** of 18 and 12:

$$lcm(18, 12) = 36.$$

In the problems below find the *hcf* and the *lcm* for each pair of integers.

Problem 0

> **0** 30 and 500:
>
> $hcf(30, 500) =$ $lcm(30, 500) =$

1 5 and 10:

$hcf(5, 10)$ = $lcm(5, 10)$ =

2 6 and 12:

$hcf(6, 12)$ = $lcm(6, 12)$ =

3 20 and 5:

$hcf(20, 5)$ = $lcm(20, 5)$ =

4 15 and 12:

$hcf(15, 12)$ = $lcm(15, 12)$ =

5 9 and 12:

$hcf(9, 12)$ = $lcm(9, 12)$ =

6 15 and 20:

hcf(15, 20) =   lcm(15, 20) =

7 16 and 24:

hcf(16, 24) =   lcm(16, 24) =

8 20 and 30:

hcf(20, 30) =   lcm(20, 30) =

9 108 and 162:

hcf(108, 162) =   lcm(108, 162) =

10 a A bus company has 21-seater and 35-seater buses.
   What is the smallest size group that would fit exactly into a
   whole number of buses *of either type?*

b A 36×60 rectangle is to be cut into equal squares, that are
   to be as large as possible.
   How large is each square?
   How many squares are there?

C12 Word problems *B*

Tackling word problems is the simplest, and one of the most important, ways to learn to *use* elementary mathematics. Each problem is given in words, so

◎ you have to read it carefully (from the beginning)

◎ sort out what you have to do

◎ extract the information from the problem as stated

◎ do the necessary calculation to get the required answer.

Problem 0

> **0** There are 14 drawing pins in box A and 27 drawing pins in box B.
>
> **a** How many drawing pins should be moved from box B to box A so that there are 3 more drawing pins in box B than in box A?
>
> **b** How many drawing pins should be moved from box B to box A so that there are 3 more drawing pins in box A than in box B?

1 Sue and Toni had 19 coins between them. After Toni had given Sue two coins, Toni had one more coin than Sue.
How many coins did Toni have at first?

2 When I shared a box of sweets between 15 children, each child received 12 sweets.
How many sweets would each child have received if the same box had been shared between 20 children?

3 Di is the youngest of three sisters. The age difference between the eldest sister and the second sister is 2 years 6 months, and the difference between the second sister and Di is 3 years 9 months. Di is now 9 years 10 months old.
How old is her eldest sister?

4 How many 20 cm by 30 cm carpet tiles are needed to cover a 5 m by 6 m rectangular floor?

5 A jug is $\frac{1}{5}$ full. When 120 ml of water is added, the jug is $\frac{3}{10}$ full.
What is the capacity of the jug?

6 The total of the ages of a father, his daughter and his two sons is
96 years. The daughter's age is half the father's age and twice
the age of each of her two brothers.
How old is the father?

7 A carpet measuring 4 m by 3 m covers 60 % of the floor area in
a rectangular room.
What is the width of the room if the length is 5 m?

8 A shopkeeper bought a stock of apples on Tuesday evening.
She sold $\frac{1}{4}$ of these apples on Wednesday, $\frac{1}{6}$ on Thursday and
$\frac{3}{8}$ on Friday. On Saturday she had 60 apples remaining.
How many apples did she buy on Tuesday?

9 My mother is twenty-six years older than I am. Next year she will
be three times as old as me.
How old am I (in years)?

10 Ducks come in three types: normal ducks – with two legs; lame
ducks – with one leg; and sitting ducks – with no legs. 100 ducks
have 100 legs between them.
Which are there more of: normal ducks or sitting ducks?
Explain your answer.

C13 Multiplication: Decimals *B* NC

Many effective strategies in mathematics are rooted in the simple idea of borrowing and then paying back what you have borrowed.

For example:　**a**　$997 + 2003 = (997 + 3) + (2003 - 3)$
$$= \underline{\quad} + \underline{\quad}$$
$$= \underline{\quad}$$

　　　　　　b　$25 \times 4004 = (25 \times 4) \times (4004 \div 4)$
$$= \underline{\quad}$$

　　　　　　c　$2.5 \times 40 \ = (2.5 \times 10) \times (40 \div 10)$
$$= 25 \times 4$$
$$= \underline{\quad}$$

Multiplying and dividing by 10, or by 100, or by 1000 is easy, so we use this to turn decimal arithmetic into integer arithmetic.

Problem 0

0　Calculate 0.037×0.3

◎　First multiply each decimal by 10, or by 100, or by 1000, ... to turn it into an integer.

$0.037 \times 10 \ \ = \underline{\quad}$　　　　　　　　$0.3 \times 10 = \underline{\quad}$

$0.037 \times 100 \ = \underline{\quad}$

$0.037 \times 1000 = \underline{\quad}$

◎　Then work out 37×3 using column multiplication

$$\begin{array}{r} 3\,7 \\ \times\ 3 \\ \hline \\ \end{array}$$

◎　Finally work backwards to decide where to put the decimal point.

$$0.037 = (0.037 \times 1000) \div 1000$$
$$= 37 \div 1000$$
$$\text{and} \quad 0.3 = (0.3 \times 10) \div 10$$
$$= 3 \div 10$$
$$\therefore \ \mathbf{0.037 \times 0.3} = (37 \div 1000) \times (3 \div 10)$$
$$= (37 \times 3) \div 10\,000$$
$$= \underline{\quad} \div 10\,000$$
$$= 0.0111$$

Use the same method to work out these decimal multiplications.

1 3.7×3 =

2 3.7×0.03 =

3 0.037×0.3 =

4 1.1×1.1 =

5 0.11×1.1 =

6 9.1×1.1 =

7 0.91×0.011 =

8 1.3×0.77 =

9 82.3×1.5 =

10 0.823×0.015 =

11 0.97×5.6 =

12 9.7×0.056 =

13 0.0097×0.56 =

14 0.0953×5.7 =

15 9.53×0.057 =

16 90.09×3.7 =

17 0.9009×3.7 =

18 5.439×14.3 =

19 0.5439×1.43 =

20 0.049×158.73 =

C14 Flexible fractions

CORE

The exercises here will help you to think flexibly when simplifying and recognising equivalent fractions.

It is easy to see that $\frac{1}{2} = \frac{3}{6}$.

It is slightly harder to recognise that $\frac{18}{36} = \frac{1}{2}$,

or to find the missing denominator/numerator in

$$\frac{18}{36} = \frac{36}{\Box} \text{ or } \frac{25}{35} = \frac{\Box}{14}.$$

Problem 0

> **0** Find the missing numerators and denominators.
>
> **a** $\frac{18}{24} = \frac{\Box}{16} = \frac{24}{\Box}$
>
> **b** $\frac{36}{54} = \frac{\Box}{36} = \frac{54}{\Box}$

Notice that we make no distinction between proper and improper fractions: when calculating you should always write $\frac{3}{2}$ **not** $1\frac{1}{2}$.

1 $\frac{\Box}{6} = \frac{15}{18} = \frac{25}{\Box}$

6 $\frac{\Box}{10} = \frac{9}{15} = \frac{15}{\Box}$

2 $\frac{\Box}{15} = \frac{36}{45} = \frac{16}{\Box}$

7 $\frac{\Box}{28} = \frac{36}{84} = \frac{15}{\Box}$

3 $\frac{\Box}{12} = \frac{12}{18} = \frac{18}{\Box}$

8 $\frac{\Box}{16} = \frac{15}{24} = \frac{25}{\Box}$

4 $\frac{\Box}{8} = \frac{15}{12} = \frac{25}{\Box}$

9 $\frac{\Box}{21} = \frac{10}{14} = \frac{35}{\Box}$

5 $\frac{\Box}{15} = \frac{24}{18} = \frac{16}{\Box}$

> **10** How many solutions are there to this problem?
>
> $\frac{\Box}{12} = \frac{\Box}{42} = \frac{15}{\Box}$

C15 Which is larger? NC

Which would you rather be given?

£$\frac{5}{9}$ or £0.59

£(27×29) or £(28^2)

Of course, you could ask your teacher, or reach for your calculator. But if you did, this would suggest that you have not yet developed the 'feeling for number' that is needed to handle numbers responsibly. Numbers are like explosives: if you treat them carelessly, they may blow up in your face!

Problem 0

> 0 Which is larger (and how can you decide quickly)?
>
> a 0.9×0.9 or 0.8
>
> b $\frac{5}{9}$ or 0.59
>
> c 27×29 or 28^2

Compare the two numbers in each question by doing *exact* calculations *in your head* (that is, without resorting to guesswork, or 'guestimation') and write down the larger one.

1 1.1×1.1,   2.2

2 1000, 25×50

3 $\frac{8}{9}$,   0.89

4 1.7, 1.3×1.3

5 $\left(\frac{9}{4}\right) \times 40$,   80

6 39×41,   1600

7 $\sqrt{1000}$,   30

8 $100 \div 7.5$,   12

9 $\frac{640}{9}$,   70

10 1.1×1.1,   1.2

11 $\left(\frac{25}{12}\right) \times 54$, 200

12 2.8×2.8, 2.7×2.9

13 49, $\sqrt{2500}$

14 $\frac{(360 + 8)}{4}$, $10(10 - 0.8)$

15 900, 29×31

CORE

73

C16 Missing digits *C* NC

If you know your tables well, and think carefully, you should be able to work out the missing digits in these calculations. There may be more than one solution, so keep alert and make sure you find all possibilities.

Problem 0

0 Find the missing digits in this multiplication.

```
      2 ☐
   ×    7
   ───────
   ☐ ☐ 9
```

Find the missing digits.

1
```
     8 ☐
  ×    4
  ───────
  ☐ 4 4
```

2
```
     ☐ 6
  ×    ☐
  ───────
  ☐ 2 8
```

3
```
   ☐ 3 ☐
  ×    6
  ───────
  ☐ 3 4
```

4
```
   ☐ 4 7
  ×    ☐
  ─────────
  1 ☐ ☐ 6
```

5
```
        5 4
  8)☐ 3 ☐
```

6
```
        ☐ 3
  7)5 ☐ ☐
```

7
```
      6 ☐ 1 ☐
  7)☐ 5 6 ☐ 6
```

8
```
      8 5 ☐
  3)2 ☐ ☐ 7
```

74

C17 Triangles

The tasks in this section involve drawing and measuring. You should of course carry out each construction as accurately as possible. But this section is not just an exercise in drawing, it is about *mathematics*. So your main job is to try to understand *why* things work out as they seem to.

Problem 0

0   Draw a line segment *AC* and mark its midpoint *M*. Draw any line segment *BD* passing through the point *M* such that *M* is the midpoint of *BD* and *BD* ≠ *AC*.

   a Measure *AB*; measure *CD*.
      What do you notice?
      Explain your answer.

   b Measure ∠*ABM*; measure ∠*CDM*.
      What do you notice?
      Explain your answer.

   c Measure ∠*BAM*; measure ∠*DCM*.
      What do you notice?
      Explain your answer.

The first observation you made in problem 0a is an example of an important property of triangles – namely the *SAS congruence criterion*.

In the two triangles △*MAB* and △*MCD*

○ the sides *MA* and *MC* match up exactly (*M* is the *i**oi*** of *AC*)

○ the two angles ∠*AMB* and ∠*CMD* are equal (*e**i*a*** o**o*i*e* angles)

○ the sides *MB* and *MD* match up exactly (*M* is the *i**oi*** of *BD*).

The SAS congruence criterion then guarantees that the two triangles are 'equal in all respects'.

One consequence of this congruence criterion is the fact that the base angles of any isosceles triangle are equal.

1   Draw a circle with centre *O*. Mark two points *A*, *B* lying on your circle.

   a Measure ∠*OAB*.   **b** Measure ∠*OBA*.

   What do you notice? Explain your answer.

2 Draw a line segment *AC* and mark the point *M* one-third of the way along *AC*. Mark a point *B* not on the line *AC* and extend *BM* to a point *D* such that $MD = 2 \times BM$.

   a Measure *AB*; measure *CD*.
      What do you notice?

   b Measure ∠*ABM*; measure ∠*CDM*.
      What do you notice?

   c Measure ∠*BAM*; measure ∠*DCM*.
      What do you notice?

3 Draw a line segment *AC* and mark a point *M* somewhere between *A* and *C*. Draw a line through *M* perpendicular to *AC*; let *B* be a point (≠ *M*) on this perpendicular.

   a Measure ∠*MBA*.

   b Construct a point *D* on *BM* produced (that is, on the line *BM* extended beyond *M*) such that ∠*MCD* = ∠*MAB*.

   c Measure *AM*, *BM*, *AB*. Measure *CM*, *DM*, *CD*.

   d Calculate the ratios *AM* : *BM* and *CM* : *DM*.
      What do you notice?

   e Calculate *AM* : *CM*, *BM* : *DM*, *AB* : *CD*.
      What do you notice?

For the remaining problems you need a sheet of square dotty paper.

4 Mark three points *A*, *B*, *C* on square dotty paper as shown on the right.

   a Suppose you measure ∠*ABC*.
      What should you find? Explain your answer.

   b Suppose you measure ∠*ACB*.
      What should you find? Explain your answer.

5 Mark three points *A*, *B*, *C* on square dotty paper as shown on the right.

   a Suppose you measure ∠*BAC*.
      What should you find? Explain your answer.

   b Suppose you measure ∠*ABC*.
      What should you find? Explain your answer.

   c Suppose you measure ∠*ACB*.
      What should you find? Explain your answer.

   d Mark the point *D*.
      What do you know about the quadrilateral *ABDC*?
      Explain your answer.

6 Mark two points *A*, *B* on square dotty paper as shown on the right.

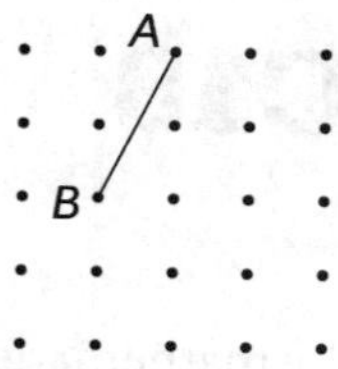

   a Explain how to choose a point *C* so that *ABC* is a right-angled isosceles triangle with a right angle at *B*.

   b Explain how to choose a point *D* so that *ABCD* is a square.

7 Mark three points *A*, *B*, *C* on square dotty paper as shown on the right.

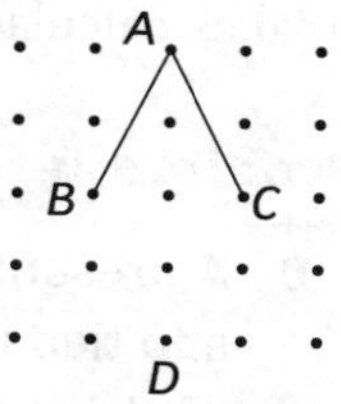

   a Suppose you measure ∠*ABC*, ∠*ACB*.
      What should you find?
      Explain your answer.

   b Mark the point *D*.
      What do you know about the quadrilateral *ABDC*?
      Explain your answer.

8 Mark three points *A*, *B*, *C* on square dotty paper as shown on the right.

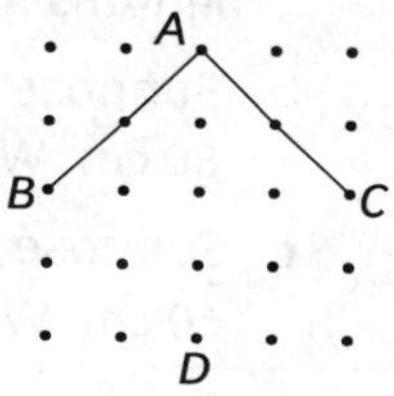

   a Suppose you measure ∠*BAC*.
      What should you find?
      Explain your answer.

   b Suppose you measure ∠*ABC*.
      What should you find?
      Explain your answer.

   c Suppose you measure ∠*ACB*.
      What should you find?
      Explain your answer.

   d Mark the point *D*.
      What do you know about the quadrilateral *ABDC*?
      Explain your answer.

9 Mark two points *A*, *B* on square dotty paper as shown on the right.

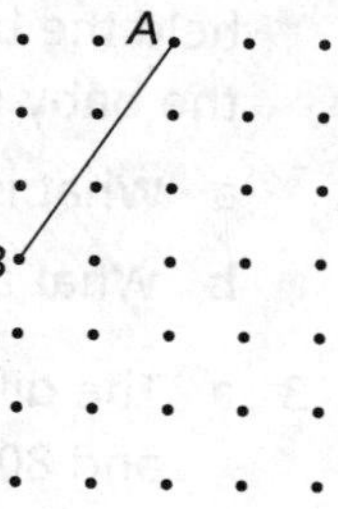

   a Explain how to choose a point *C* so that *ABC* is a right-angled isosceles triangle with a right angle at *B*.

   b Explain how to choose a point *D* so that *ABCD* is a square.

C18 Weighing the baby

In mathematics you learn how to calculate. But you also need to *think*. A simple idea often helps to uncover hidden information in a way that makes calculation easier.

Problem 0

0 A present in a box (a cuboid) is wrapped and tied up with string, with one loop of string in each of the three possible directions (as shown).

a Suppose the three loops of string have lengths 40 cm, 60 cm, 60 cm. What is the volume of the box?

b Suppose the three loops of string have lengths 40 cm, 60 cm, 80 cm. What is the volume of the box?

c Suppose the three loops of string have lengths 40 cm, 50 cm, 60 cm. What is the volume of the box?

1 I have three mathematical cats called *x*, *y* and *z*.
x and *y* together weigh 7 kg. *y* and *z* together weight 8 kg.
z and *x* together weigh 11 kg.

a What would my cats weigh if I weighed all three together?

b What are the individual weights of my three cats?

2 Weighing the baby at the clinic was a problem. The baby would not keep still and caused the scales to wobble. So I held the baby and stood on the scales while the nurse read 78 kg. Then the nurse held the baby while I read off 69 kg. Finally I held the nurse while the baby read off 137 kg.

a What is the combined weight of all three?

b What are the three individual weights?

3 a The different faces of a cuboid have perimeters 40 cm, 60 cm and 80 cm. Find its length, breadth and height.

b The different faces of a cuboid have perimeters 40 cm, 50 cm and 60 cm. Find its length, breadth and height.

c The different faces of a cuboid have perimeters 30 cm, 50 cm and 70 cm. Find its length, breadth and height.

One curry and one cup of tea cost £4. Two curries and two ice creams cost £9. One ice cream and one cup of tea cost £2.

   a What would one curry, one cup of tea and one ice cream cost?

   b What does each item cost separately?

A child's box of bricks contains cubes, cones and spheres. On a two-pan balance two cones and a sphere exactly balance one cube; one cube and one sphere exactly balance three cones.
How many spheres will exactly balance a single cone?

On a simple two-pan balance, 7 golden dollrs exactly balance 13 silver nickls, and 7 silver dims exactly balance 13 golden dollrs. How many silver coins will exactly balance 100 golden dollrs?

Tables have four legs, stools have three legs, people have two legs.

   a On Saturday evening when we all sat down to supper there were no empty places and there were 44 legs altogether at the table.
How many people were there?

   b When we all sat down to Sunday lunch, there were again no empty places and there were 55 legs altogether.
What did we eat? (Was it lamb or mutton?)

A cuboid has faces with perimeters 6 cm, 8 cm, 10 cm. Calculate the lengths of the edges of the cuboid, its total surface area, and its volume.

You are given a cuboid.

   a Suppose the different faces have areas 20 cm^2, 24 cm^2 and 30 cm^2. What is the volume of the box and what are the lengths of the edges?

   b Suppose the different faces have areas 36 cm^2, 60 cm^2 and 135 cm^2. What is the volume of the box and what are the lengths of the edges?

You are given a cuboid with total surface area 400 cm^2.

   a Suppose the base of the cuboid is 4 cm by 8 cm. What is its height?

   b Suppose the base of the cuboid is 4 cm by 14 cm. What is its height?

   c Suppose the base of the cuboid is 8 cm by 12 cm. What is its height?

C19 Areas

You should know how to find the area of a rectangle and of a triangle.

Problem 0

0 *ABCD* is a rectangle. How can I

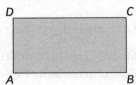

   a draw a straight line through the point *A* to divide the rectangle into two parts with equal area?

   b draw a straight line through the point *A* to cut off one-quarter of the total area?

   c draw a straight line through the point *A* to cut off one-third of the total area?

1 a A rectangle has length 8 cm and area 5 cm^2.
     What is its height?

   b A rectangle has length 1.2 cm and area 0.75 cm^2.
     What is its height?

2 A rectangle *ABCD* has length 6 cm and height 4 cm. The point *P* is two-thirds of the way along *DC*.

   a Find the area of triangle *APB*.

   b Find the area of triangle *ADP* and triangle *BCP*.

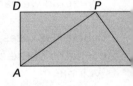

3 In the shape shown here all the angles are right angles.
Calculate the area enclosed.

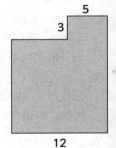

4 *ABC* is a given triangle.
How can you

    a draw a straight line through the point *A* to divide the triangle into two parts with equal area?

    b draw a straight line through the point *A* to cut off one-quarter of the total area?

    c draw a straight line through the point *A* to cut off one-third of the total area?

5 In triangle *ABC* the point *M* is the mid-point of *AB*.
How can you

    a draw a straight line through the point *M* to divide the triangle into two parts with equal area?

    b draw a straight line through the point *M* to cut off one-quarter of the total area?

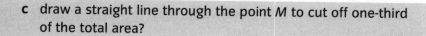

    c draw a straight line through the point *M* to cut off one-third of the total area?

6 In the rectangle *ABCD* the point *M* is the mid-point of *AD*.
How can you

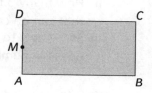

    a draw a straight line through the point *M* to divide the rectangle into two parts with equal area?

    b draw a straight line through the point *M* to cut off one-quarter of the total area?

    c draw a straight line through the point *M* to cut off one-third of the total area?

C20 Tiling *B*

In a *tiling* you have to cover a large shape with copies of a given *tile*. The tiles must fit edge-to-edge, with no overlap. If the large shape can be completely covered, the tiling is *complete*. Sometimes a complete tiling is impossible.

Problem 0

0 Suppose you have a large supply of 3 by 1 rectangles.

a You want to tile a 3 by 3 square.
How many 3 by 1 tiles do you need?

b Suppose you want to tile a 4 by 4 square.

i What is the smallest possible number of 1 by 1 squares that remain uncovered?

ii How many 3 by 1 tiles do you need to cover the squares that can be covered?

iii Show how to tile a 4 by 4 square leaving the minimum possible number of squares uncovered.

1 a Show how to tile a 6 by 6 square with 3 by 1 tiles.

b Show how to tile a 9 by 9 square with 3 by 1 tiles.

2 When you 'almost tile' a 4 by 4 square with 3 by 1 tiles, how many possible locations are there for the empty square(s)?

3 Suppose you want to tile a 5 by 5 square with 3 by 1 tiles.

a What is the smallest possible number of squares that remain uncovered?

b How many 3 by 1 tiles do you need?

c Show how to tile a 5 by 5 square with 3 by 1 tiles leaving the minimum possible number of squares uncovered.

d When you 'almost tile' a 5 by 5 square with 3 by 1 tiles, how many possible locations are there for the empty square(s)?

4 Suppose you want to tile a 7 by 7 square.

   a What is the smallest possible number of 1 by 1 squares that remain uncovered?

   b How many 3 by 1 tiles do you need?

   c Show how to tile a 7 by 7 square leaving the minimum possible number of squares uncovered.

   d When you 'almost tile' a 7 by 7 square with 3 by 1 tiles, how many possible locations are there for the empty square(s)?

5 a For which values of n is it possible to tile an n by n square completely with 3 by 1 tiles?
(In problem **0a** you showed how to tile a 3 by 3 square.
How could you use this to *prove* that an n by n square can always be tiled for all the larger values you have specified?)

   b In questions 2 and 3 you showed that when $n = 4$ or $n = 5$ it is possible to 'almost tile' an n by n square with 3 by 1 tiles – leaving just ___ square(s) uncovered.
How would you *prove* that the same is true for all values of n not included in part a?

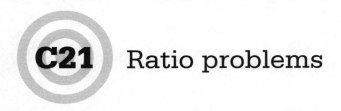

C21 Ratio problems

Problems involving the idea of *ratio* depend on simple arithmetic; but be prepared to read the problem and think what to do in order to solve it.

Problem 0

> **0** On a map, a distance of 5 km on land is represented by 1 cm on the map.
>
> **a** A forest has area 50 km².
> What is the area of the corresponding part of the map?
>
> **b** On the map a park has area 4 cm².
> What is the actual area of the park?

1 I pack 51 boxes of peaches with 16 peaches in each box.
How many boxes would I use if I put only 12 peaches in each box?

2 When a tank is two-thirds full it contains 120 litres.
How much does it contain when it is three-quarters full?

3 It takes me 21 minutes to walk to work at 6 km per hour.
How long would it take me if I could manage 7 km per hour?

4 A car uses 8 litres of petrol for 48 km.
How far could it travel on 20 litres of petrol?

5 A man weighs 70 kg when he is 20 years old.
How much will he weigh when he is 60?

6 **a** If $\frac{3}{4}$ of a given number is 12, what is $\frac{3}{2}$ of the same number?

b If $\frac{4}{5}$ of a given number is 12, what is $\frac{4}{3}$ of the same number?

7 A haystack contains enough hay to feed 12 horses for 15 days.
For how many days could the same haystack feed 20 horses?

8 I am making a $\frac{1}{150}$ scale model of a railway steam engine.
If the original engine is 12 m long, how long will my model be?

9 Two numbers are in the ratio 7 : 3.
If their difference is 24, what are the two numbers?

10 In a class of 30 pupils the ratio of boys to girls is $2:3$.

   a If 6 girls (and no boys) join the class what is the new ratio of boys to girls?

   b How does this new ratio change if 2 boys (and no girls) then leave the class?

11 Four points, A, B, C, D, in order along a straight line are such that $AB = 2 \times BC = CD$.
   What fraction is BD of AD?

12 The latest *Decimalisation Decree* states that each day is to be divided into 10 *new hours*, each new hour is to be divided into 100 *new minutes*, and each new minute is to be divided into 100 *new seconds*.
   Which is longer, an old second or a new second?
   Calculate the ratio 'new second : old second'.

13 In a band the ratio of woodwind players to brass players is $3:4$.
   The ratio of woodwind to brass and strings combined is $2:5$.
   What is the ratio of woodwind players to string players?

14 100 cm^3 of copper weighs 892 g.
   What would a 12 cm × 6 cm × 5 cm cuboid of copper weigh?

C22 Measures and decimal arithmetic

Amounts of money, such as £1.30, are usually written in decimal form (provided you are careful to write one pound and five pence as £1.05!).

Other measurements often have to be *changed* into decimal form before you can carry out a calculation efficiently (using decimal arithmetic – either in your head or in written form using long multiplication).

Problem 0

> **0 a** What would it cost to buy 1 m 20 cm of gold wire at £10 per metre?
>
> **b** What would 1 m 20 cm of gold wire cost
>
>   **i** at £9.90 per metre?
>
>   **ii** at £10.10 per metre?
>
>   **iii** at £9.80 per metre?
>
>   **iv** at £10.20 per metre?
>
> **c** What would 1 m 35 cm of gold wire cost at a price of £9.60 per metre?

If the numbers are 'nice' (as in part **b**), you may be able to see a simpler approach without converting measurements into decimal form and multiplying; but as soon as the numbers get more awkward (as in part **c**), it may be easier to use decimal multiplication.

1 m at £9.60 per metre costs £(1×9.60) = £9.60

$\frac{1}{2}$ m at £9.60 per metre would cost £$\left(\frac{1}{2} \times 9.60\right)$ = £___

0.35 m at £9.60 per metre costs £(0.35×9.60) = £___

1.35 m at £9.60 per metre costs £(1.35×9.60)

$$
\begin{array}{r}
1\ 3\ 5 \\
\times\ \ \ 9\ 6 \\
\hline
8\ 1\ 0 \\
1\ 1\ 2\ 5\ 0 \\
\hline
\end{array}
$$

∴ Cost = £___

1　**a**　What would 500 g of salami cost if priced at £ 1.30 per 100 g?

　　b　What would 500 g of salami cost if priced at £ 1.35 per 100 g?

　　c　What would 960 g of salami cost if priced at £ 1.35 per 100 g?

2　**a**　What would it cost if a taxi journey 5 km long was charged at a rate of £ 2 per km?

　　b　**i**　What would it cost if a taxi journey 5 km 200 m long was charged at a rate of £ 2 per km?

　　　　ii　What if the same taxi journey was charged at the rate of £ 1.90 per km?

　　c　What would it cost if a taxi journey 5 km 400 m long was charged at a rate of £ 2.35 per km?

3　**a**　What would it cost if a phone call lasting 7 minutes was charged at a rate of 5 p per minute?

　　b　**i**　What would it cost if a phone call lasting 7 minutes 30 seconds was charged at a rate of 5 p per minute?

　　　　ii　What if the same phone call was charged at 4.7 p per minute?

4　**a**　**i**　How far would I travel if I drove at 30 mph for 90 minutes?

　　　　ii　How far would I travel if I drove at 32.4 mph for 90 minutes?

　　b　**i**　How far would I travel if I drove at 28 mph for 75 minutes?

　　　　ii　How far would I travel if I drove at 28.4 mph for 75 minutes?

　　c　**i**　How far would I travel if I drove at 30 mph for 45 minutes?

　　　　ii　How far would I travel if I drove at 32.4 mph for 45 minutes?

5　**a**　What would it cost to carpet a floor 4 m by 3 m if carpet costs £ 25 per square metre?

　　b　What would it cost to carpet a floor 4.2 m by 2.8 m if carpet costs £ 37.50 per square metre?

6　How much does a pane of glass measuring 75 cm by 80 cm cost if it is priced at £ 6.30 per square metre?

C23 Where did the money go? *B* NC

Calculating is relatively straightforward: the ingredients and the recipe are given; you then have to combine them correctly to get the answer.

Solving problems is often more like detective work: you are given the outcome, and must then work out how it was obtained.

Problem 0

> **0** I bought some Swizzles and some Stickies for 48 p. Swizzles cost 9 p each; Stickies cost 4 p each. How many of each did I buy?

1 Swizzles cost 9 p each; Stickies cost 4 p each.
If I buy four Swizzles and nine Stickies, how much change will I get from £ 1?

2 a I bought three of my favourite chocolate bars. I gave the cashier a whole number of pounds and received 2 p change. How much would four bars cost?

   b I bought seven of my favourite packets of mints. I gave the cashier a whole number of pounds and received 3 p change. How much would three bars cost?

3 a I spent £ 2 on 10 p and 20 p stamps. I bought three times as many 10 p stamps as 20 p stamps.
How many of each stamp did I buy?

   b A package cost £ 5 to post. Each stamp used was either a 50 p stamp or a 10 p stamp. There were five times as many 10 p stamps as 50 p stamps.
How many of each kind did I use?

   c A package cost £ 6 to post. Each stamp was either a 50 p stamp or a 10 p stamp. I used the same number of each kind.
How many 10 p stamps did I use?

   d A package cost £ 8 to post. Each stamp was either a 20 p stamp or a 10 p stamp. I used twice as many 10 p stamps as 20 p stamps.
How many 10 p stamps did I use?

4 If 15 Euros are worth the same as 20 Afros, and 25 Afros are worth the same as 30 Chinos, how many Euros would you expect to get for 40 Chinos?

5 I spent £10 on some eggs direct from a friendly farmer. Extra large eggs cost 50 p each; medium-sized eggs cost 10 p each; small eggs cost 5 p each. For two of these sizes I bought the same number of eggs.
How many eggs of each size did I buy?

6 Three friends earned £300 by cutting lawns. They reckoned that John did one and a half times as much work as Mark and Ben combined, and that Mark did one and a half times as much work as Ben.
How much of the money should go to Ben?

7 I spent £20 on some fish. Each goldfish cost £1.80; each angel fish cost £1.40.
How many of each type did I buy?

8 I spent £5 on a mixture of chocolate bars and fruit bars. Chocolate bars cost 26 p and fruit bars cost 18 p.
How many of each did I buy?

C24 Highest common factors and least common multiples *B* NC

The *highest* common factor (or *hcf*) of 12 and 18 is 6: $hcf(12,18) = 6$.

The *least* common multiple (*lcm*) of 12 and 18 is 36: $lcm(18,12) = 36$.

Problem 0

0 a Find the *hcf* and *lcm* of 66 and 99:
$$hcf(66, 99) = \underline{\quad}; \qquad lcm(66, 99) = \underline{\quad}.$$

  b Find the *hcf* and *lcm* of 135 and 189:
$$hcf(135, 189) = \underline{\quad}; \qquad lcm(135, 189) = \underline{\quad}.$$

To find the *hcf* and *lcm* of two integers: find the *hcf* first. For example:

To find $hcf(135, 189)$, look for common factors.
  2 is not an option (since 135 is o**).
  So try 3:
$$135 = 3 \times 45 = 3 \times 3 \times 15 = 3 \times 3 \times 3 \times 5 = \underline{27} \times 5;$$
$$189 = 3 \times 63 = 3 \times 3 \times 21 = 3 \times 3 \times 3 \times 7 = \underline{27} \times 7.$$
  $\therefore$ $hcf(135, 189) = \underline{27}$.
$$135 = 5 \times \underline{27}, \qquad 189 = \underline{27} \times 7.$$
  $\therefore$ $lcm(135, 189) = 5 \times \underline{27} \times 7.$

Find the *hcf* and *lcm* of each pair of integers.

1 48 and 60: $hcf(48, 60)$ = $lcm(48, 60)$ =

2 48 and 112: $hcf(48, 112)$ = $lcm(48, 112)$ =

3 60 and 108: $hcf(60, 108)$ = $lcm(60, 108)$ =

4 66 and 264: $hcf(66, 264)$ = $lcm(66, 264)$ =

5 63 and 105: $hcf(63, 105)$ = $lcm(63, 105)$ =

6 135 and 450: $hcf(135, 450)$ = $lcm(135, 450)$ =

7 144 and 252: $hcf(144, 252)$ = $lcm(144, 252)$ =

8 252 and 324: $hcf(252, 324)$ = $lcm(252, 324)$ =

9 168 and 252: $hcf(168, 252)$ = $lcm(168, 252)$ =

10 126 and 294: $hcf(126, 294)$ = $lcm(126, 294)$ =

25 Fractions and decimals   NC

You should know that $\frac{3}{10}$ is the same as $\frac{30}{100}$ or $\frac{300}{1000}$.

When you write 375, the 3 stands for 3×100
the 7 stands for 7×10
the 5 stands for 5×1.

When you write 0.375, the 3 stands for $3 \times \frac{1}{10}$
the 7 stands for $7 \times \frac{1}{100}$
the 5 stands for $5 \times \frac{1}{1000}$

This means that it is easy to turn a decimal into a fraction.

$$0.375 = \frac{3}{10} + \frac{7}{100} + \frac{5}{1000}$$
$$= \frac{300}{1000} + \frac{70}{1000} + \frac{5}{1000} = \frac{375}{1000}$$

However, if you want to *recognise* $\frac{375}{1000}$, it is essential to simplify by cancelling common factors in the numerator and denominator:

$375 = 3 \times \underline{\quad}$; $1000 = 8 \times \underline{\quad}$;

$\therefore 0.375 = \frac{375}{1000} = \frac{\square}{\square}$

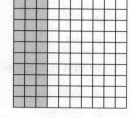

$$\frac{3}{10} = \frac{30}{100}$$

CORE

Problem 0

a Which (simplified) fraction has decimal 0.75? Explain.

b Find the exact decimal for $\frac{7}{25}$.

c Which (simplified) fraction has decimal 0.125?

d Find the exact decimal for $\frac{3}{40}$.

Copy and complete:

a $\frac{13}{5} = 2 + \frac{\square}{5}$

b $4\frac{1}{2} = \square \times \frac{1}{2}$

c $6.805 = 6 + \frac{8}{\square} + \frac{5}{1000}$

d $6 \times \frac{4}{5} = \frac{4}{5} + \square \times \frac{4}{5}$

In problem 0a: $0.75 = \dfrac{\square}{100} = \dfrac{3 \times \square}{4 \times \square} = \dfrac{\square}{\square}$.

Use the same idea to answer these questions.

2 Which (simplified) fraction has decimal

    a 0.2   **c** 0.5   **e** 0.8

    b 0.4   **d** 0.6   **f** 2.4?

3 Which (simplified) fraction has decimal

    a 0.04   **c** 0.36   **e** 0.74

    b 0.375   **d** 0.625   **f** 0.875?

4 Which (simplified) fraction has decimal

    a 1.25   **c** 2.35   **e** 5.125

    b 3.6   **d** 0.008   **f** 3.75?

In problem 0b: $\dfrac{7}{25} = \dfrac{7 \times \square}{25 \times \square} = \dfrac{\square}{100} = 0.\underline{\quad}$

Use the same idea to answer these questions.
Do *not* use a calculator.

5 Work out the exact decimals for these fractions.

    a $\dfrac{1}{5}$ **d** $\dfrac{3}{5}$ **g** $\dfrac{24}{5}$

    b $\dfrac{2}{5}$ **e** $\dfrac{6}{5}$

    c $\dfrac{4}{5}$ **f** $\dfrac{12}{5}$

6 Work out the exact decimals for these fractions.

    a $\dfrac{1}{20}$ **d** $\dfrac{11}{20}$ **g** $\dfrac{5}{20}$

    b $\dfrac{3}{20}$ **e** $\dfrac{21}{20}$ **h** $\dfrac{8}{20}$

    c $\dfrac{7}{20}$ **f** $\dfrac{4}{20}$ **i** $\dfrac{2}{20}$

7 Work out the exact decimals for these fractions.

    a $\dfrac{1}{25}$ **d** $\dfrac{4}{25}$ **g** $\dfrac{44}{25}$

    b $\dfrac{2}{25}$ **e** $\dfrac{5}{25}$ **h** $\dfrac{1}{40}$

    c $\dfrac{3}{25}$ **f** $\dfrac{11}{25}$ **i** $\dfrac{7}{40}$

The simplest application of arithmetic is to problems involving measures.

Problem 0

0 Yesterday my champion snail, *Nippy*, crawled 40 cm 8 mm in 36 seconds.

    a At this pace (if he could keep it up), how far would *Nippy* crawl in 1 hour?

    b At the same pace, how far would *Nippy* crawl in 1 day?

    c At the same pace, roughly how long would *Nippy* take to crawl 1 km?

1 A horse covers 2.5 km in 5 minutes.

    a What is the horse's speed in km/h?

    b How long does the horse take to run 1 km?

2 A car travels at 30 m per second.

    a How far will the car travel in 1 minute?

    b What is the car's speed in km/h?

    c How long will the car take to travel 1 km?

3 How many 65 cm lengths of tape can I cut from a roll 9 m 10 cm long?

4 A motorcyclist travels at 40 m/sec.

    a Calculate the distance he travels in 5 seconds.

    b How long will he take to cover 1 km?

    c Calculate his speed in km/h.

5 18 litres of milk is poured into 30 cl glasses. How many glasses can be filled?

6 750 g of meat cost £9.60.

    a What does 1 kg of meat cost?

    b How much would 700 g cost?

7   A cyclist travels 50 km in two and a half hours.

   a   How far does the cyclist travel in 1 minute?

   b   What is the speed of the cyclist in km/h?

8   A horse covers 2.6 km in 5 minutes.

   a   What is the horse's speed in km/h?

   b   What is the horse's speed in m/sec?

   c   How long does the horse take to run 1 km?

9   A baker uses 14 kg of flour to make 175 rolls.

   a   How much flour does he need to make 35 rolls?

   b   How many rolls can he make with 4.8 kg of flour?

   c   How many rolls can he make with 1 kg of flour?

   d   How much flour is needed for each roll?

10 Yesterday my champion snail, *Nippy*, crawled 40 cm 8 mm in 36 seconds.

   a   Write in decimal form: 36 seconds = ___ hours

                           40 cm 8 mm = ___ metres.

   b   What single arithmetical calculation should I do with the two answers in part **a** to re-calculate how far *Nippy* would crawl in 1 hour (assuming that he could keep going at this speed)?

CORE

Problem 0

> **0** Joshua rolls one large ball at five skittles – numbered 1, 2, 3, 4, 5. His *total score* is the sum of the numbers on the skittles knocked down.
>
> **a** How many ways are there to knock down just *one* skittle? How many different totals can you get if just *one* skittle falls down?
>
> **b** How many ways are there to knock down exactly *three* skittles? How many different totals can you get?

The answer to problem **0a** is obvious: the five skittles all have different values, so there are ___ ways to knock down just one skittle. Each way gives a different score, so there are ___ different scores.

Problem **0b** is harder; you need a reliable *method* to list *all* possibilities.

1 a i How many different ways are there to knock down exactly *five* skittles?

   ii How many different total scores are there if all *five* skittles are knocked down?

  b i How many different ways are there to knock down exactly *zero* skittles?

   ii How many different total scores are there if *zero* skittles are knocked down?

  c When I *knock down* 5 skittles, I *leave* 0 skittles standing.
When I *knock down* 0 skittles, I *leave* 5 skittles standing.
That is, the number of ways to choose 5 skittles to *knock down* is equal to the number of ways to choose 5 skittles to *leave standing*!
How does this explain why the answers to **a** and **b** have to be equal?

2 a i How many different ways are there to knock down exactly *one* skittle?

  ii How many different total scores are there if just *one* skittle is knocked down?

 b i How many different ways are there to knock down exactly *four* skittles?

  ii How many different total scores are there if *four* skittles are knocked down?

 c When I *knock down* 4 skittles, I *leave* ___ skittle standing. When I *knock down* 1 skittle, I *leave* ___ skittles standing. How does this explain why the answers to **a** and **b** have to be equal?

3 a i How many different ways are there to knock down exactly *two* skittles?

  ii How many different total scores are there if just *two* skittles are knocked down?

 b i How many different ways are there to knock down exactly *three* skittles?

  ii How many different total scores are there if *three* skittles are knocked down?

 c When I *knock down* 3 skittles, I *leave* ___ skittles standing. When I *knock down* 2 skittles, I *leave* ___ skittles standing. How does this explain why the answers to **a** and **b** have to be equal?

4 Make a table collecting the answers to problems **1–3**.

Number of skittles knocked down	0	1	2	3	4	5
Number of different ways to do this	1					
Number of different total scores	1					

5   There is a clever way to complete the third row in the table of problem **4** (though problem **6** shows that it is not quite as easy as it may seem at first sight).

   a If 0 skittles are knocked down, the only possible total score is ___.

   b If just 1 skittle is knocked down, the smallest possible score is ___ and the largest possible score is ___.
      Because of the way the skittles are numbered, I can get *any total in between* these two values.

   c If 2 skittles are knocked down, the smallest possible score is ___ + ___, and the largest possible score is ___ + ___.
      How can I be sure that with 2 skittles, I can get *all possible scores in between* these two values?

   d If 3 skittles are *knocked down*, the total score is
      $(1 + 2 + 3 + 4 + 5) -$ (total of the two skittles *left standing*).
      So by part **c** I get all values between
      $(1 + 2 + 3 + 4 + 5) - (4 + 5)$ and $(1 + 2 + 3 + 4 + 5) - (1 + 2)$,
      that is, all values between ___ and ___.

6   Now let the skittles be numbered 2, 3, 5, 7, 11 instead of 1, 2, 3, 4, 5.
   Suppose that 3 skittles are knocked down.

   a How many different ways are there to knock down 3 skittles?

   b What is the largest possible total score (if just 3 skittles are knocked down)?
      What is the smallest possible total score?
      How many different total scores are there if just 3 skittles are knocked down?

E1 How many solutions?   NC

'8 ☐' stands for a two-digit integer. '4 ☐' is another two-digit integer. How many different solutions are there to this equation?

'8 ☐' – '4 ☐' = 39

The first thing to notice is that '4 ☐' cannot be equal to 40. Why not?

If '4 ☐' = 41, then '8 ☐' = ___.
If '4 ☐' = 42, then '8 ☐' = ___.

And so on. So how many solutions are there?

Problem 0

0 How many solutions are there to each equation?

a '8 ☐' – '4 ☐' = 38

b '8 ☐' – '4 ☐' = 31

c '7 ☐' – '4 ☐' = 31

How many solutions are there to each equation?

1 '2 ☐' – '1 ☐' = 10

2 '3 ☐' – '2 ☐' = 10

3 '4 ☐' – '3 ☐' = 11

4 '4 ☐' – '3 ☐' = 9

5 '5 ☐' – '4 ☐' = 19

6 '6 ☐' – '5 ☐' = 20

7 '8 ☐' – '6 ☐' = 10

8 '8 ☐' – '6 ☐' = 11

9 '8 ☐' – '6 ☐' = 19

10 '8 ☐' – '6 ☐' = 20

11 '8 ☐' – '6 ☐' = 21

12 '8 ☐' – '6 ☐' = 29

13 '8 ☐' – '4 ☐' = 50

14 '8 ☐' – '4 ☐' = 48

15 '8 ☐' – '4 ☐' = 32

16 '8 ☐' – '4 ☐' = 30

17 '☐ 2' – '☐ 1' = 10

18 '☐ 2' – '☐ 1' = 11

19 '☐ 2' – '2 ☐' = 10

20 '☐ 2' – '2 ☐' = 43

21 '☐ 3' – '☐ 7' = 36

22 '☐ 7' – '☐ 1' = 36

EXTENSION

1 How big is the angle marked *y*?

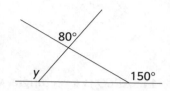

2 *ABC* is an isosceles right-angled triangle. Find its three angles (in degrees).

3 What is the angle between the two hands of a clock at 20:15?

4 Calculate ∠*ABD* in the figure below.

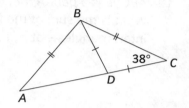

5 *ABCDE* is a regular pentagon. *P* is a point inside the pentagon such that triangle *ABP* is equilateral.
Calculate ∠*APE*.

6 a Find a time when the angle between the two hands of a clock is exactly 170°.

b Find another time when the angle between the two hands of a clock is exactly 170°.

7 *ABCDEFGH* is a regular octagon.
Find the angles of triangle *ACE*.

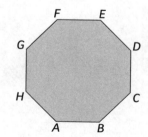

8 Diagonals *AC* and *BD* of rectangle *ABCD* cross at *X*.
If ∠*AXD* = 20°, find ∠*ACB*.

9 *ABCDEF* is a regular hexagon. *AE* and *DF* cross at *X*.
What size is ∠*AXD*?

EXTENSION

10 Calculate the angle marked *x* in the diagram.

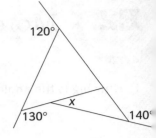

11 ABCD is a rectangle with AB twice as long as BC. X is a point such that ABX is an equilateral triangle that overlaps the rectangle ABCD. M is the midpoint of BX.
What size is ∠CMB?

12 ABCDE is a *pentagram* (or star pentagon).
What is the sum of the five marked interior angles – at A, at B, at C, at D and at E?

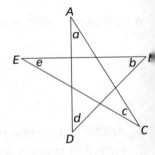

13 a In triangle ABC, ∠BAC = 80° and the exterior bisectors of the angles at B and at C meet at E.
What is the size of ∠BEC?

b In triangle ABC, ∠BAC = y° and the exterior bisectors of the angles at B and at C meet at E.
What is the size of ∠BEC?

E3 Arithmetic to ponder NC

1 Evaluate 432 432 ÷ 1001

2 Evaluate 12 345 679 × 9

3 Evaluate
111 111 111 + 22 222 222 + 3 333 333 + 444 444 + 55 555 + 6666 + 777 + 88 + 9.

4 Evaluate

  a 1 + 3 + 5 + 7 + 9

  b 1 + 3 + 5 + 7 + 9 + 11

  c 1 + 3 + 5 + 7 + 9 + 11 + 13

5 **a** Our maths teachers, Mr and Mrs B. East, made us calculate their
favourite sum. We had to add up the six 3-digit integers that
can be made using the digits 1, 2, 3 once each.
Write the answer in the form 2 × ___ (so that Mr and Mrs B. East
can each have half of the answer).

  b Suppose you were to add up all the 4-digit integers that can be
made using the digits 1, 2, 3, 4 once each.
Explain why the sum must be equal to 'six times *ten thousand,
ten hundred and tenty-ten*'.

6 How many of these expressions are equal to 25?

  $1 + 2 \times 3 - 4 \times 5$

  $1 \times 2 + 3 \times 4 + 5$

  $1 + 2 \times 3 \times 4$

  $1 + 2 \div 3 + 4 \times 5$

  $2 + 3 \times 4 + 5$

7 1 + 2 = ___
4 + 5 + 6 = ___ + ___
9 + 10 + 11 + 12 = ___ + ___ + ___
16 + 17 + 18 + 19 + 20 = ___ + ___ + ___ + ___

8 **a** Work out $\frac{1}{2} \times \frac{2}{3} \times \frac{3}{4} \times \frac{4}{5} = \boxed{}$.

  b In last year's exams, half of the class got As. One-third of the
rest got Bs. One-quarter of the remainder got Cs. One-fifth of
the others got Ds.
What fraction of the class got Es or worse?

9 a Work out $\dfrac{1}{1\times2} + \dfrac{1}{2\times3} + \dfrac{1}{3\times4} = \boxed{}$.

   b Work out $\dfrac{1}{1\times2} + \dfrac{1}{2\times3} + \dfrac{1}{3\times4} + \dfrac{1}{4\times5} = \boxed{}$.

10 A millionth of a second is called a *microsecond*.
Roughly how long is a *microcentury*?

11 Calculate $3^2 + 4^2 = \underline{}^2$; $3^3 + 4^3 + 5^3 = \underline{}^3$.

12 a Which numbers are represented by these seven different
expressions?

   i $\dfrac{1}{(11 - 2)}$ **iv** $\dfrac{1234}{(11\,111 - 5)}$ **vii** $\dfrac{1\,234\,567}{(11\,111\,111 - 8)}$

   ii $\dfrac{12}{(111 - 3)}$ **v** $\dfrac{12\,345}{(111\,111 - 6)}$

   iii $\dfrac{123}{(1111 - 4)}$ **vi** $\dfrac{123\,456}{(1\,111\,111 - 7)}$

   b Write the next three expressions that continue this sequence,
and calculate their numerical values.

13 $2 \times 3 - 1 \times 4 =$
$3 \times 4 - 2 \times 5 =$
$4 \times 5 - 3 \times 6 =$
$5 \times 6 - 4 \times 7 =$

14 $3 \times 4 - 1 \times 5 =$
$4 \times 5 - 2 \times 6 =$
$5 \times 6 - 3 \times 7 =$
$6 \times 7 - 4 \times 8 =$

15 $6 \times 7 =$
$66 \times 67 =$
$666 \times 667 =$

16 a Choose any 3-digit integer, '*abc*' with $a \neq c$. Reverse the order
of the digits ('*cba*') and subtract the smaller 3-digit integer from
the larger.
Treat the result as a 3-digit integer (possibly with hundreds
digit equal to 0), reverse the order of the digits and add.
Write down the 4-digit answer.

   b Multiply the 4-digit answer to **a** by 9.
What do you notice?

   c Calculate 33^2 and 99^2.

1 a Find three prime numbers such that the sum of all three is
       also a prime number.

   b Find three more prime numbers such that the sum of all
       three is also a prime number.

2 Suppose I count 1, 2, 3, . . . out loud.
   Which is the first number I say that will contain the letter 'a'?

3 Find the sum of all prime numbers between 20 and 120 which
   are one more than a multiple of 5.

4 Find an integer less than 100 which is increased by 20 % when
   its digits are reversed.

5 Find the sum of all prime numbers <120 which are 1 more
   than a multiple of 7.

6 a Find three positive integers such that the sum of any two
       of them is a perfect square.

   b Find another three such positive integers.

7 The product of three consecutive integers is 990.
   What is their sum?

8 a Find three different two-digit prime numbers such that the
       average of any two of them is also a prime number.

   b Do there exist three two-digit prime numbers such that the
       average of any two of them is prime and the average of all three
       is also prime?

9 a You are told that one of the integers in a list of distinct positive
       integers is 97 and that their average value is 47. If the sum of
       all the integers in the list is 329, what is the largest possible
       value for a number in the list?

   b Suppose you are not told the value of the sum of all the
       numbers in the list. What is the largest possible number in the
       list then?

10 Find the smallest multiple of 9 that has no odd digits.

EXTENSION

11 a Find the smallest positive integer with exactly three factors (including itself and 1). Find the second smallest such integer. How many such integers are there ≤ 20.

b Find the smallest positive integer with exactly four factors (including itself and 1).
Find the second smallest such integer.
Find the third smallest such integer.
How many such integers are there ≤ 20?

c Find the smallest positive integer with exactly five factors (including itself and 1).
Find the second smallest such integer.

d Find the smallest positive integer with exactly six factors (including itself and 1).
Find the second smallest such integer.
Find the third smallest such integer.

e Find the smallest positive integer with exactly seven factors.
Find the second smallest such integer.

12 a 6 is called a *perfect* number, because when you add up all its factors you get exactly double the number you started with:
$1 + 2 + 3 + 6 = 12$. (Alternatively, the sum of all the 'proper factors' of 6 – that is, those factors strictly less than 6 itself – is exactly equal to 6.)

    i Find the next perfect number after 6.

    ii Check that 496 is a perfect number (in fact, the third smallest perfect number).

b i 8 is called a *deficient* number, because when you add up all its proper factors you get a number smaller than the number you started with: $1 + 2 + 4 = 7$. How many deficient numbers are there < 50?

    ii 12 is called an *abundant* number, because when you add up all its proper factors you get a number larger than the number you started with: $1 + 2 + 3 + 4 + 6 = 16$. How many abundant numbers are there < 50?

In this section you have to share a number of identical circular cakes between a given number of people.

The problems combine the need to work flexibly with fractions with the exercise of visual imagination in two dimensions.

Only consider cuts in which each piece of cake is a *sector* of one of the circular cakes, and forms a fractional part of that cake.

The goal here is to create *identical portions*; that is, the cakes have to be cut up so that everyone receives their fair share *in an identical way*, with different people receiving identical-looking portions.

This is easy if you can choose the number of pieces to use.
If there are c cakes,
  cut each cake into as many equal parts as there are people,
  then give each person c of these parts.

The problem becomes more interesting if you have to use fewer (or more) pieces.

a Show how to divide 2 cakes into 4 pieces, so that 4 people each receive *identical portions*.

b Show how to divide 2 cakes into 8 pieces, so that 4 people each receive *identical portions*.
Can you find more than one way of doing this?

c Show how to divide 2 cakes into 12 pieces, so that 4 people each receive *identical portions*.
Find two different solutions.

a Is it possible to divide 2 cakes into 3 pieces, so that 3 people each receive *identical portions*?

b Show how to divide 2 cakes into 6 pieces, so that 3 people each receive *identical portions*.
Can you find more than one way of doing this?

c Show how to divide 2 cakes into 9 pieces, so that 3 people each receive *identical portions*.
Find two different ways of doing this.

3 a Is it possible to divide 2 cakes into 5 pieces, so that 5 people each receive *identical portions*?

b Show how to divide 2 cakes into 10 pieces, so that 5 people each receive *identical portions*.
Find three different ways of doing this.

c Show how to divide 2 cakes into 15 pieces, so that 5 people each receive *identical portions*.
Find two different ways of doing this.

4 a Show how to divide 3 cakes into 8 pieces, so that 4 people each receive *identical portions*.
Can you find more than one way of doing this?

b Show how to divide 3 cakes into 12 pieces, so that 4 people each receive *identical portions*.
Find three different ways of doing this.

5 Show how to divide 3 cakes into 10 pieces, so that 5 people each receive *identical portions*.
Find two different ways of doing this.

6 Show how to divide 5 cakes into 12 pieces, so that 6 people each receive *identical portions*.
Can you find more than one way of doing this?

1   For how many two-digit numbers is the sum of the digits a multiple of 6?

2   As everyone knows a normal cat has 18 claws – 5 on each front leg and 4 on each back leg. At *Sam's Sanctuary for Mangled Moggies* there are four three-legged cats, each with a different leg missing.
How many claws do they have between them?

3   In a class of 30 pupils there are 22 pupils who are right-handed and there are 14 girls.
What is the smallest number of girls who could be right-handed?

4   How many positive integers ≤ 100 can be written as the product of two even integers?

5   a   A regular pentagon *ABCDE* can be cut into three triangles, all of whose vertices are vertices of the regular pentagon.
In how many different ways can this be done?

    b   A regular hexagon *ABCDEF* can be cut into four triangles, all of whose vertices are vertices of the regular hexagon.
In how many different ways can this be done?

6   Find a pair of prime numbers which, between them, use each of the four digits, 1, 2, 3 and 4, exactly once.
How many different pairs are there?

7   If I take the two-digit number, 46, reverse the order of the digits and add, I get a total of 110.
How many two-digit starting numbers give the total 99?

8   In how many different ways can I pay 10 p using standard British coins?

9   How many two-digit prime numbers remain prime when their digits are reversed?

0   In how many different ways can 105 be written as the sum of two or more consecutive positive integers?

1   How many three-digit square numbers remain three-digit squares when their digits are reversed?

12 An urn contains 100 balls: 28 red, 20 green, 12 yellow, 20 blue, 10 white and 10 black.
How many balls must you draw from the urn to be sure that you will get 15 balls of the same colour?

13 In how many different ways can you pay 20 p using standard British coins?

14 A sequence of terms chosen from the numbers, 1, 2, 3, 4, 5, 6, 7 and 8, is such that the second term is bigger than the first, and each term after that is greater than the sum of the two previous terms.
How many possible sequences of this kind are there with at least three terms?

15 The years 1999 and 2002 both use just two different digits. How many years since 1AD (up to today) have used just two different digits?

E7   What's my number? *B*   **NC**

1   **a**   I am thinking of a number less than 50. It is a multiple of 7 and its digits differ by 2.
How many possibilities are there for my number (and what could it be)?

    b   I am thinking of a number less than 80. It is a multiple of 7 and its digits differ by 3.
How many possibilities are there for my number (and what could it be)?

2   **a**   I am thinking of a number less than 50. It is 3 more than a multiple of 7 and 7 more than a multiple of 3.
How many possibilities are there for my number?

    b   I am thinking of a number less than 100. It is 3 more than a multiple of 7 and 7 more than a multiple of 3.
How many possibilities are there for my number now?

3   **a**   I am thinking of a number less than 50. It is 6 more than a multiple of 5 and 5 more than a multiple of 6.
How many possibilities are there for my number?

    b   I am thinking of a number less than 100. It is 6 more than a multiple of 5 and 5 more than a multiple of 6.
How many possibilities are there for my number now?

4   **a**   I am thinking of a number less than 50. It is 4 more than a multiple of 5 and 5 more than a multiple of 4.
How many possibilities are there for my number?

    b   I am thinking of a number less than 100. It is 4 more than a multiple of 5 and 5 more than a multiple of 4.
How many possibilities are there for my number now?

5   **a**   I am thinking of a number less than 50. It is 3 more than a multiple of 4, 4 more than a multiple of 5, and 5 more than a multiple of 3.
How many possibilities are there for my number?

    b   I am thinking of a number less than 100. It is 3 more than a multiple of 4, 4 more than a multiple of 5, and 5 more than a multiple of 3.
How many possibilities are there for my number now?

E X T E N S I O N

6 a I am thinking of a number less than 50. It is a multiple of 4, and the sum of its digits is an odd prime.
How many possibilities are there for my number?

b I am now thinking of a number less than 100. It is a multiple of 4, and the sum of its digits is an odd prime.
How many possibilities are there for my number?

7 a I am thinking of a number less than 50 with exactly three odd factors. The sum of its digits is 9.
How many possibilities are there for my number?

b I am now thinking of a number less than 100 with exactly three odd factors. The sum of its digits is 9.
How many possibilities are there for my number?

8 a I am thinking of a number less than 50 with exactly three odd factors. The sum of its digits is a prime number.
How many possibilities are there for my number?

b I am now thinking of a number less than 100 with exactly three odd factors. The sum of its digits is a prime number.
How many possibilities are there for my number?

E8 Beginnings and ends   NC

Standard procedures are important. But the power of mathematics lies in the way elementary methods can be used to tackle *unfamiliar* problems. The problems in this section may appear slightly unusual. Don't be surprised if you are not sure how to proceed; the challenge is to use what you know to solve the problems as efficiently and as completely as you can.

1 a i Find a positive integer such that when an extra digit '2' is written at the beginning (left-hand end) of the number you get five times the number you started with.

 ii How many such integers are there?
 How are they all related?

b i Find a positive integer such that when an extra digit '2' is written at the beginning of the number you get six times the number you started with.

 ii How many such integers are there?
 How are they all related?

c i Find a positive integer such that when an extra digit '2' is written at the beginning of the number you get nine times the number you started with.

 ii How many such integers are there?
 How are they all related?

2 a i Find a positive integer such that when an extra digit '1' is written at the beginning of the number you get six times the number you started with.

 ii How many such integers are there?
 How are they all related?

b i Find a positive integer such that when an extra digit '1' is written at the beginning of the number you get five times the number you started with.

 ii How many such integers are there?
 How are they all related?

EXTENSION

c i Find a positive integer such that when an extra digit '1' is written at the beginning of the number you get nine times the number you started with.

ii How many such integers are there?
How are they all related?

Each of us will approach these problems differently. Look for efficient ways of searching: for example, in problem **1a** you are told that a 2-digit integer is five times some other integer – so it must have units digit ___ or ___. As the problems get more complex, try to *improve* the efficiency of your search (and resist any temptation to resort to a machine search – which usually produces *answers* without *insight*).

3 Find a two-digit integer such that when the units digit and tens digits are interchanged, the number becomes 20 % bigger.

4 Find a two-digit integer such that when the units digit and tens digits are interchanged, the number becomes 75 % bigger.
How many such two-digit integers are there?

5 Find a two-digit integer such that when the units digit and tens digits are interchanged, the number becomes $62\frac{1}{2}$ % smaller.

6 Find a two-digit integer such that when the units digit and tens digits are interchanged, the number is $4\frac{1}{2}$ times bigger.

A *crossnumber* is like a crossword, but with digits in place of letters. One digit goes in each small square, and no answer begins with a '0'.

1 Find all possible solutions to this crossnumber, and prove that you have found them all.

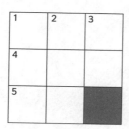

CLUES

Across	Down
1. Cube	1. Cube
3. Square	2. Prime
5. Square	4. Square

2 Find all possible solutions to this crossnumber, and prove that you have found them all.

CLUES

Across	Down
1. Multiple of 3	1. Cube
3. Cube	2. Square
4. Cube	3. Cube

3 Find all possible solutions to this crossnumber, and prove that you have found them all.

CLUES

Across	Down
1. 7 × 5A	1. As easy as '123'
4. Square of 3D	2. Even
5. Multiple of 19	3. Multiple of 13

EXTENSION

113

4 Find all possible solutions to this crossnumber, and prove that you have found them all.

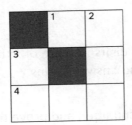

CLUES

Across
1. See 3D
3. Cube
4. 5 times 3D

Down
2. Square
3. 4 times 1A

5 Find all possible solutions to this crossnumber, and prove that you have found them all.

CLUES

Across
1. Square
4. Palindrome
5. Even

Down
1. Square
2. Square palindrome
3. Digits go up in 2s

Positive integers are usually written using

◎ the digits 0–9 and

◎ powers of 10 in our *base 10* numeral system.

For example,

$$2734_{base\ 10} = 2 \times 10^3 + 7 \times 10^2 + 3 \times 10 + 4$$

Integers can also be written in other bases, for example, using the digits 0–1 and powers of 2 in *base 2*

$$2734_{base\ 10} = 2048 + 512 + 128 + 32 + 8 + 4 + 2$$
$$= 1 \times 2^{11} + 1 \times 2^9 + 1 \times 2^7 + 1 \times 2^5 + 1 \times 2^3 + 1 \times 2^2 + 1 \times 2$$
$$= 10101010111_{base\ 2}$$

or using the digits 0–8 and powers of 9 in *base 9*

$$2734_{base\ 10} = 3 \times 729 + 6 \times 81 + 6 \times 9 + 7$$
$$= 3 \times 9^3 + 6 \times 9^2 + 6 \times 9 + 7$$
$$= 3667_{base\ 9}$$

1 Write these numbers in *base 10*.

  a $303_{base\ 6}$ = ____ *base 10*   **c** $515_{base\ 8}$ = ____ *base 10*

  b $201_{base\ 7}$ = ____ *base 10*

2 Write these *base 10* numbers in the specified base.

  a $63_{base\ 10}$ = ____ *base 2*   **c** $400_{base\ 10}$ = ____ *base 7*

  b $85_{base\ 10}$ = ____ *base 2*   **d** $1885_{base\ 10}$ = ____ *base 12*

3 Carry out the addition shown here in *base 8*.
(Do not change the summands into *base 10*; use the
standard addition algorithm – collecting 8s instead of 10s.)

$$\begin{array}{r} 3\,5\,2\,3\,5_{base\ 8} \\ +\,1\,7\,0\,6\,4_{base\ 8} \\ \hline _{base\ 8} \end{array}$$

4 Carry out the subtraction shown here in *base 8*.
(Do not change the summands into *base 10*; use the
standard subtraction algorithm – with 8s instead of 10s.)

$$\begin{array}{r} 7\,7\,2\,6\,0_{base\ 8} \\ -\,6\,4\,7\,1\,3_{base\ 8} \\ \hline _{base\ 8} \end{array}$$

5 Carry out the multiplication shown here in *base 8*.
(Do not change the summands into *base 10*; use the standard algorithm – carrying 8s instead of 10s.)

$$\begin{array}{r} 1\ 4\ 6\ 3_{base\ 8} \\ \times \qquad 5_{base\ 8} \\ \hline base\ 8 \end{array}$$

6 Carry out the multiplication shown here in *base 8*.
(Do not change the summands into *base 10*; use the standard algorithm – carrying 8s instead of 10s.)

$$\begin{array}{r} 2\ 5\ 2\ 5\ 2\ 5_{base\ 8} \\ \times \qquad 3_{base\ 8} \\ \hline base\ 8 \end{array}$$

7 a Jenny sorted fifteen 1 p coins into four bags. To remind herself what each bag was worth, she wrote on each bag the number of coins in that bag. She could then pay every amount from 1 p to 15 p exactly, without opening any bag and without needing change.
What numbers were on the four bags?

b Suppose Jenny wanted to be able to pay (directly, without opening up any of her bags and without receiving change) every amount from 1 p up to 31 p.
How many more bags would she need to make up?

8 a Suppose you wanted to design a set of *standard* weights for use with a set of *balance pans* (where the object to be weighed is put in one pan and is balanced by standard weights in the other pan). If you wish that every whole number of grams from 1 g up to 1 kg can be balanced exactly, you could use 1000 standard weights of 1 g, but this would not be very efficient. Could you get by with just 100 standard weights?
What would be the most efficient choice of standard weights to use?

b The system described in part **a** is based on *addition*: to weigh a 74 g object, you need a combination of standard weights that *add* to 74 g.
A more subtle system would allow you to place standard weights in *both* pans and to use *subtraction*: a 3 g object could then be weighed exactly by using standard 1 g and 4 g weights (placing the standard 4 g weight in one pan and the object and the standard 1 g weight in the other pan: the weight of the object would then be 4 g – 1 g = 3 g).
What would be the most efficient set of standard weights to use in such a system?

Fractions, ratio and pre-algebra

1 My Christmas present cost £ 2.30 plus half its price.
What did it cost?

2 When a barrel is 30 % empty it contains 30 gallons more than when it is 30 % full.
How many gallons does the barrel hold when full?

3 A book is opened at random. The product of the two visible page numbers is 4160.
What are the numbers on the two pages?

4 One-third of the people at a party are women, a quarter are girls, one-sixth are men, and there are six boys.
How many people are there at the party?

5 Which provides the bigger share, three bars of chocolate shared between five, or four bars of chocolate shared between seven?

6 A primary school has 380 pupils of whom 70 % can swim. If 40 % of the boys cannot swim and 200 girls can swim, how many girls are there in the school?

7 When standing part way up a ladder, a painter notices that there are twice as many rungs above the rung he is standing on as there are below it. After climbing 8 more rungs the number of rungs above his rung is equal to the number below it.
How many rungs are there on the ladder?

8 In a school the ratio of boys to girls is 2 : 3, and the ratio of girls to teachers is 8 : 1.
What is the ratio of students to teachers?

9 a What is the largest amount of money less than £ 1 that I can have in standard British coins without being able to pay exactly 40 p?

b What is the largest amount of money less than £1 that I can have in standard British coins without being able to pay exactly 50p?

10 On my necklace the ratio of red beads to blue beads is 2 : 3.
   The ratio of red beads to yellow beads is 4 : 3.
   What is the ratio of red beads to the rest?

11 Two rectangles have equal perimeters.

   a If the first rectangle has sides in the ratio 2 : 5, while the
      second has sides in the ratio 3 : 4, what is the ratio of their
      areas?

   b If the first rectangle has sides in the ratio 3 : 5, while the
      second has sides in the ratio 1 : 3, what is the ratio of their
      areas?

   c If the first rectangle has sides in the ratio 3 : 5, while the
      second has sides in the ratio 5 : 7, what is the ratio of their
      areas?

12 Fifteen jumps are as long as fourteen steps; eight steps are as
   long as nine skips; twenty-one skips are as long as twenty hops.
   How many hops are as long as one jump?

13 Fresh apricots have a *moisture content* of 80 %. When left in the
   sun to dry they lose 75 % of their moisture content. What is the
   moisture content of sun-dried apricots?

14 Take any two-digit integer. Subtract the sum of its digits. Then
   divide the answer by 9.
   What do you find?
   Explain your answer.

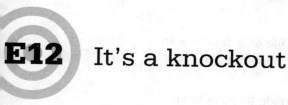

E12 It's a knockout

Problem 0

> **0** The third round of the FA Cup always has 64 teams – including the 44 teams in the Premier League (20) and the Championship (24) together with another 22 teams who have won through from preliminary rounds.
>
> After the *third* round, there are the *fourth* round, the *fifth* round, the *quarter finals*, the *semi-finals* and the *final*.
>
> Starting with the 64 teams in the third round, how many matches does it take (ignoring replays) to produce the eventual cup winners?

1 In a knockout competition with 4 teams, the first round would also be the 'semi-final'. So it would take just ***ee matches to produce a winner.

Suppose there were 7 teams. One team could be given a bye to the second round, while the other 6 teams competed for the other three semi-final places.

How many matches would it take altogether to produce an eventual winner?

2 Imagine a knockout competition with 9 teams entering. The first round could then involve just one match – leaving 8 teams to compete in the next round.

So starting with 9 teams, how many matches would it take altogether to produce an eventual winner?

3 How would you plan a knockout competition with 10 teams entering?

How many matches would it take to produce an eventual winner?

4 a Suppose 100 teams entered a knockout competition.

How many teams would you want in the second round?
So how many matches should there be in the first round?

b How many matches would it take altogether to produce an eventual winner?

5 In conker arithmetic, each conker starts out life as a '0-er' – with *value* 0. When an '*m*-er' destroys an '*n*-er', it becomes an '$(m + n + 1)$-er'.

    a Suppose I have a '5-er'. How many conkers in all have been destroyed in all the matches that have contributed to my conker's value of 5?

    b Suppose I have a '50-er'. How many conkers must have been destroyed in all the matches that have contributed to my conker's value of 50?

6 The figure shows a 2×3 bar of chocolate, which I want to break into 6 separate pieces using straight breaks.

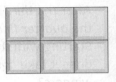

    a One way would be to split it into two 3s, and then break each 3-er using two breaks, making a total of $1 + 2 \times 2 = \underline{}$ breaks in all.

    b Another way would be to split the bar into three 2s, and then break each 2-er with a single break, making a total of $2 + 3 \times 1 = \underline{}$ breaks in all.

7 The figure shows a 3×4 bar of chocolate, which I want to break into 12 separate pieces using straight breaks.

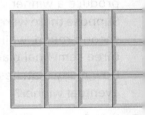

    a One way would be to split it into three 4s, and then break each 4-er using breaks, making a total of $2 + 3 \times 3 = \underline{}$ breaks in all.

    b Another way would be to split the bar into four 3s, and then break each 3-er with two breaks, making a total of $3 + 4 \times 2 = \underline{}$ breaks in all.

8 **a** Imagine a knockout competition with N teams entering. Explain how each knockout match eliminates $\underline{}$ team. Hence conclude that the number of matches required to produce an eventual winner is '$\underline{} - 1$'.

    b Imagine an $m \times n$ chocolate bar which you want to break into $m \times n$ separate pieces. Explain how each break increases the number of pieces by $\underline{}$. Conclude that, no matter what sequence of breaks is used, the number of breaks required is '$\underline{} - 1$'.

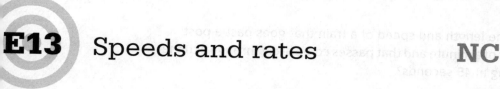

E13 Speeds and rates   NC

1 A man walks 200 metres per minute.
   How long will he take to walk 6 km?

2 Petra cycled from A to B. She took $\frac{3}{4}$ hour to cycle one-quarter
   of the distance at 16 km/h. She covered the remaining distance
   at 12 km/h and arrived at B at 10:30 am.
   When did she leave A?

3 At 2:20 pm a van left town X for town Y, averaging 40 mph.
   At 2:30 pm a car left Y for X on the same road, averaging 60 mph.
   The car arrived in X at 3:30 pm.
   When did the van arrive at Y?

4 A cyclist and a walker are 30 km apart and are approaching
   each other. The cyclist travels at 15 km/h and the walker
   at 5 km/h.
   After how long do they meet? And where?

5 A man takes half an hour to walk downhill to the bus stop
   in the morning on his way to work, and an hour to walk the
   same distance uphill in the evening on his way home.
   The difference between his two average speeds is 4 km/h.
   How far is his house from the bus stop?

6 An express delivery man averages 60 mph on the outward
   journey from A to B, but on the return journey the traffic is
   heavy and he only averages 40 mph.
   What was his average speed for the complete round trip?

7 A slow train is travelling at 30 km per hour. A dog walks from
   the front of the train towards the rear at 100 metres per minute.
   A flea on the back of the dog hops from head to tail at 10 mm
   per second.
   How much does the flea's position in space change in 30 seconds?

8 What is the length and speed of a train that goes past a post in quarter of a minute and that passes completely through a tunnel 540 m long in 45 seconds?

9 If five mice can eat five pounds of cheese in five minutes, how long would it take 99 mice to eat 99 pounds of cheese?

10 To get from home to school I have to cycle one mile up a hill and one mile down the other side. One day I get up late and leave myself only 10 minutes for the whole journey.

    a What must my average speed be for the whole ourney?

    b If I average 6 mph on the way up the hill, at what speed must I go down the other side if I am to get to school on time?

11 I can only manage one step at a time on an escalator, but I can vary the speed at which I climb.
When I climb a moving up-escalator at one step per second I make 20 steps to get to the top.
When I climb the same escalator at two steps per second, I make 32 steps to reach the top.
How high is the escalator (in steps)?

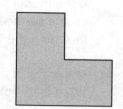

1 The L-shape shown below is made from three unit squares. The
   figure is to be cut into isosceles right-angled triangles.
   What is the smallest possible number of pieces?

2 The total length of the edges of a cube is 24 cm.
   Calculate the total surface area of the cube.

3 A rectangle with integer length sides has an area numerically
   equal to its perimeter.
   Find all possible dimensions for the rectangle.

4 A square has area 25 cm^2.
   What is the area of the circle inscribed in the square?

5 a i   A cube has surface area 150 cm^2. What is its volume?
      ii A cube has surface area 384 cm^2. What is its volume?

   b A cube has volume 216 cm^3. What is its surface area?

6 ABCD is a square. P is the mid-point of the side AB; Q is two-thirds
   of the way along the side BC; R is three-quarters of the way along
   the side CD.
   What fraction of the square is occupied by the triangle PQR?

7 The floor of a square hall is tiled with identical square tiles. Amy
   and Buz count the total number of tiles on the two diagonals: Amy
   counts 102 and Buz counts 101.
   If only one of them is right, who is it and how many tiles are there
   on the whole floor?

8 A room is 10 m square and 4 m high. A spider is in one of the
   corners on the floor and sees a fly across the room at the
   diagonally opposite corner on the ceiling.
   If the fly does not move, what is the shortest distance the spider
   must crawl in order to catch the fly?

9   *ABCD* is a square, with *L* halfway along *AB*, *M* one-third of the
    way along *BC*, and *N* one-quarter of the way along *CD*.
    What fraction of the square is occupied by triangle *LMN*?

10 Four small cubes form a model of a medallists' podium for an
    athletics championship.
    If the model podium has a volume of 108 cm^3, find the total
    visible surface area that has to be painted (that is, not
    including the bottom).

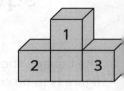

11 The faces of a cuboid have areas 24 cm^2, 32 cm^2 and 48 cm^2.
    What is its volume?

12 A fish tank in the shape of a cuboid, 50 cm long, 40 cm wide and
    20 cm high, is half-filled with water. A solid metal cube is then
    placed on the bottom of the tank.
    a   How far will the water rise if the cube has edge length 10 cm?
    b   How far will the water rise if the cube has edge length 20 cm?

More missing digits

Whenever you are given two starting numbers, you should be able to add one to the other, subtract one from the other, multiply one by the other, or divide one into the other without a calculator. And you need to be able to do this *quickly* and *reliably*.

The logic behind the arithmetical algorithms for addition, subtraction, multiplication and division leads *from* the given starting numbers *to* the answer.

But if you understand what is really going on, and are willing to *think*, you should be able to work backwards and fill in the missing digits in these puzzles.

1 Something is clearly wrong with these additions! In fact every digit is wrong – but they are all just 'one out'. Can you put them right?

a
```
    4 3
  + 5 7
  ─────
  2 0 7
```

b
```
  7 6 6 8
 +2 6 9 2
 ────────
  9 0 2 7
```

2 Something is clearly wrong with this multiplication! In fact every digit is wrong – but they are all just one out. Can you put things right?

```
    1 6 6 3
  ×       3
  ─────────
  2 1 3 7 9
```

3 In each of these divisions, one of the given digits is wrong. Decide which it must be and work out all the missing digits.

a
```
         □ 2
  5 □ ) 5 □ □ □
        □ □ □
        ─────
          □ □
          □ 9
```

c
```
          8 □
  □ 2 ) □ □ 6
        □ 5
        ───
        □ □
        □ □
```

b
```
         2 □
  4 □ ) □ □ □ 8
       □ □ □
       ─────
         □ □
         6 □
```

d
```
          7 □
  □ 5 ) □ □ □
        □ □
        ───
        □ □ □
        □ □ 8
```

4 In these divisions, most of the digits are missing. But you should be able to work out what they are.

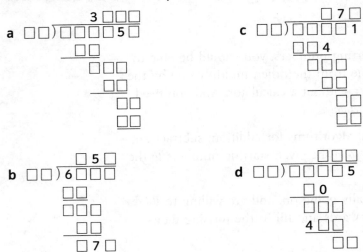

E16 Painting polyhedra

Thinking in three dimensions is important in mathematics and in many of its applications. We live in three dimensions, but there is not much for beginners to actually *calculate* in three dimensions. This section gives you the chance to think and imagine things in two and three dimensions as part of a challenge to count the number of 'different' figures one can create by painting familiar geometrical shapes with two colours – say *red* and *blue*.

We begin by painting the vertices of certain regular polygons.

1   How many different figures can one create by painting each of the three *vertices* of an equilateral triangle using just two colours – red and blue? (Two figures are treated as being *the same* if one can be turned into the other by moving it in the plane *without turning either figure over.*)

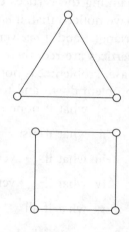

2   How many different figures can one create by painting each of the four *vertices* of a square using just two colours – red and blue? (Two figures are treated as being *the same* if one can be turned into the other by moving it in the plane *without turning either figure over.*)

3   How many different figures can one create by painting each of the six *vertices* of a regular hexagon using just two colours – red and blue? (Two figures are treated as being *the same* if one can be turned into the other by moving it in the plane *without turning either figure over.*)

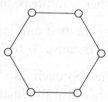

4   How many different figures can one create by painting each of the three *edges* of an equilateral triangle with one of two colours – red and blue? (Two figures are treated as being *the same* if one can be turned into the other by moving it in the plane *without turning either figure over.*)

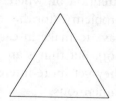

Polygons are two-dimensional: they are bounded all round by straight line segments, meeting at *vertices* (points), and enclosing a two-dimensional 'inside'.

The corresponding shapes in three dimensions are **polyhedra**; these are bounded all round by *faces* (flat polygons), meeting at *edges* (line segments) and at *vertices* (points), and have a three-dimensional 'inside'. The remaining problems consider painting the simplest polyhedra – cubes and regular tetrahedra (that is, pyramids with an equilateral triangular base, and with sloping faces which are also equilateral triangles).

Whenever a mathematical problem is too difficult to answer immediately, look for a way of breaking it into simpler parts. When painting the vertices of an equilateral triangle (problem **1**), you should have noticed that, if *no* vertices are red, there is just one possible painted triangle; and if *one* vertex is red, or if *two* vertices are red, or if all *three* vertices are red, there is still just one possible painted triangle in each case. Problem **2** is not quite so simple; but it is still helpful to break the problem down and to think first

    i   what if none of the four vertices is red; then

    ii what if just ___ vertex is red; then

    iii what if ___ vertices are red; then

    iv what if ___ vertices are red; and finally

    v what if all ___ vertices are red.

When you break the problem down like this you should notice that

◎   the first and last of these five cases are essentially the same – because "0 *e*" is just like "0 **ue".

The approach also highlights the fact that the initial cases **i** and **ii** (and hence also the final cases **iv** and **v**) are very easy to count. This focuses attention on where the real effort is needed – namely in case **iii**. In problem **2** (for the square) this is still quite easy; the only distinction you have to make in case **iii** is whether the two red vertices are *adjacent* or not). But things are not quite so simple for the regular hexagon. And they get more interesting now that we are moving on to three dimensions.

In the first two problems with polyhedra each flat *face* of the polyhedron is painted either *wholly* red or *wholly* blue and you have to find a way of counting how many differently painted figures can be produced.

5 How many different figures can one create by painting each of the four *faces* of a regular tetrahedron using just two colours – red and blue? (Two figures are treated as being *the same* if one can be rotated into the other by moving it in three dimensions.)

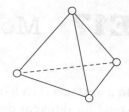

6 How many different figures can one create by painting each *face* of a cube using just two colours – red and blue? (Two figures are treated as being *the same* if one can be rotated into the other by moving it in three dimensions.)

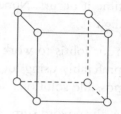

In the two final problems, it is the *vertices* that are to be painted either red or blue. In problem **4** you may have noticed that, for polygons, painting *edges* is just like painting *vertices* – because edges and vertices *alternate* as you go round the polygon (so we could swap the names edge and vertex without doing much damage). But for polyhedra, painting faces and painting vertices are quite different – though they are related in an unexpected way (via 'duality').

7 How many different figures can one create by painting each of the four *vertices* of a regular tetrahedron using just two colours – red and blue?

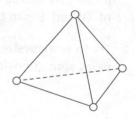

8 How many different figures can one create by painting each *vertex* of a cube using just two colours – red and blue?

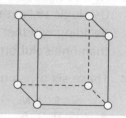

In a *word sum* each letter stands for one of the digits 0–9. Different letters stand for different digits, and each letter stands for the same digit each time it occurs. None of the integers in any of the sums starts with the digit 0.

Your job is to work out which digits the letters could stand for – preferably using logic rather than guesswork, so that you uncover all possible solutions.

A given word sum may be impossible (in which case you have to explain why it cannot have a solution); or it may have just one solution (in which case you should try to find that solution and prove that it is the only one); or it may have several solutions (in which case a logical approach, without guesswork, will uncover all possible solutions).

1 Find a solution to this word sum.
   How many different solutions can you find?
   (Note that solutions come in pairs: given any solution, the values of 'O' and 'E' can be interchanged.)

```
  T O P
+ S E T
S U M S
```

2 Try to work systematically to find all possible solutions to this word sum. (Consider the five possible values of 'A' in turn.)

```
    A D D
    A D D
+     O H
D E A R
```

3 At first sight this one feels wrong. But you can never be sure! Use logic to limit the possibilities in this multiplication before deciding whether it has no solution, just one solution, or more than one solution.

```
      T W O
×     T W O
T H R E E
```

4 These six divisions have exactly five solutions between them.

a A)2 0 0 5 → S U M

c A)2 0 0 7 → S U M

e A)2 0 0 9 → S U M

b A)2 0 0 6 → S U M

d A)2 0 0 8 → S U M

f A)2 0 1 0 → S U M

E18 Buckets and hoops

Joshua is back at the fair – this time throwing bean bags at buckets numbered 1, 2, 3, 4, 5. Each throw that lands in a bucket 'scores' the number on that bucket: the 'total score' is calculated by adding up the scores for each throw.

1 Suppose Joshua has just *one* throw.

   a What is his maximum possible score?

   b Can every score from 0 (= *i**) up to the maximum be achieved?

   c In how many different ways can each score be achieved (with just one throw)?

2 Suppose Joshua has *two* throws.

   a What is his maximum possible score?

   b Can every score from 0 (= *i**) up to the maximum be achieved?

   c In how many different ways can each score be achieved (with just two throws)?
Make a table:

Total score S	0	1	2	3	4	5	6	7	8	9	10
Number of ways of achieving score S	1										

Problem 2c raises the question of what we mean by *different* ways of achieving a given score. If we fix the total score, there are different *score patterns* that achieve the given total: the two *score patterns* '2 + 3' (that is, 'score 2 with first throw, and 3 with the second throw') and '5 + 0' (that is, 'score 5 with first throw, and 0 with the second throw') are different, though they both produce the same total score of 5.

There is another complication: when counting the number of score patterns one has to decide whether '2 + 3' and '3 + 2' count as the same or as different.
Score patterns are called *unordered* if '2 + 3' and '3 + 2' are the same; *score patterns* are called *ordered* if '2 + 3' and '3 + 2' are different.

For the moment stick to counting *unordered* score patterns. Go back and check that this is what you counted in the bottom row of your table in problem 2 (the eleven entries in the bottom row of your table should have total 31).

EXTENSION

If in problem **1** you made a table for the number of ways of achieving score S ($0 \leq S \leq 5$), the second row would look pretty uninteresting: 1, 1, 1, 1, 1, 1. But it would have displayed a feature that you may have noticed in your table in problem **2**.

3 What do you notice about the bottom row of your table in problem **2**? Can you explain (with proof) why the number of ways has this slightly surprising symmetry?

4 Suppose Joshua has *three* throws.

   a What is his maximum possible score?

   b Can every score from 0 up to the maximum be achieved?

   c In how many different (unordered) ways can each score be achieved (with just three throws)?
   Make a table:

Total score S	0	1	2	3	4	5	6	7	8	9	10	11	12	13	14	15
Number of ways of achieving score S	1															

   d What do you notice about the bottom row of your table in part **c**? Can you explain (with proof) why the number of ways has this surprising symmetry?

5 Suppose Joshua has *four* throws.

   a What is his maximum possible score?

   b Can every score from 0 up to the maximum be achieved?

   c In how many different (unordered) ways can each score be achieved (with just four throws)?
   Make a table:

Total score S	0	1	2	3	4	5	6	7	8
Number of ways of achieving score S	1								

   d What do you notice about the bottom row of your table in part **c**? Can you explain (with proof) why the number of ways has this surprising symmetry?

6 Suppose Joshua throws up to 7 bean bags at *five* buckets numbered 1, 2, 3, 4, 5.

  a How many (unordered) ways are there for him to score 3?

  b How many ways are there to score 4?

  c How many ways are there to score 5?

  d How many ways are there to score 6?

  e How many ways are there to score 7?

We end by looking at the number of *ordered* score patterns.

7 a Suppose Joshua has *two* throws.

  i How many different *ordered* 'score patterns' are there for each possible score (with just two throws)?
Make a table:

Total score S	0	1	2	3	4	5	6	7	8	9	10
No. ordered score patterns	1	2									

  ii What do you notice about the bottom row in your table? Can you explain?

b Suppose Joshua has *three* throws.

  i How many different *ordered* score patterns are there for each possible score (with just three throws)?
Make a table:

Total score S	0	1	2	3	4	5	6	7	8	9	10	11	12	13	14	15
No. ordered score patterns	1	3														

  ii What do you notice about the bottom row in your table? Can you explain?

The title of this section is *Buckets and hoops*. Buckets differ from skittles (see *Skittles A*, page 29, and *Skittles B*, page 95) in that a skittle can only be knocked down *once*, whereas with bean bags and buckets, two bean bags may land up in the same bucket. So with *skittles* each total has to be achieved without repeating any individual skittle score, but with *buckets*, a total may include repeated individual bucket scores. Fairgrounds often include games where you have to throw hoops and get them to hook onto pegs. Provided the peg is not too short, hoops are like buckets, in that they also allow repeated individual scores.

E19 More tiling: Fun with *i*o*a**i

This section looks at the numbers that emerge when you count how many different ways there are to tile certain rectangles with 2×1 rectangular tiles.

Each 2×1 tile has area ___ (square units). So the rectangle we want to tile must have e*e* area – say $2n$ square units.

The simplest rectangles with this property have height 1 and length $2n$, and each $1 \times 2n$ rectangle can be tiled using 2×1 tiles in *just one way*.

The next simplest family of rectangles with even area are $2 \times n$ rectangles. So the first really interesting question is:

How many ways are there to tile a $2 \times n$ rectangle with 2×1 tiles?

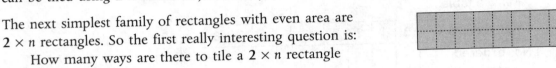

1 Suppose $n = 1$.
A 2×1 rectangle can be tiled with 2×1 tiles in exactly ___ way.

2 Suppose $n = 2$.
How many 2×1 tiles are needed to tile a 2×2 square?
A 2×2 square can be tiled with 2×1 tiles in exactly ___ ways:
(both tiles *o*i*o**a* or both tiles *e**i*a*).

3 Suppose $n = 3$.
How many different ways are there to tile a 2×3 rectangle with 2×1 tiles?

4 Suppose $n = 4$.
How many different ways are there to tile a 2×4 rectangle with 2×1 tiles?

Let R_n stand for the number of different ways of tiling a $2 \times n$ rectangle with 2×1 tiles.

5 Make a table to summarise the results of problems 1–4.

n = length of $2 \times n$ rectangle	0	1	2	3	4	5	
R_n = number of ways of tiling $2 \times n$ rectangle with 2×1 tiles							

When experimenting with small values of n accuracy is crucial; inaccurate data can only confuse you. *Care* is important, but accuracy often requires *insight* in order to make the task of counting manageable. So it may be worth going back and looking at problem 4 again – slightly differently.

6 a Count the R_4 different ways of tiling a 2×4 rectangle again. Think about how the *last* column on the right is tiled. There are just two ways of positioning the last tile:

  i the last tile could be *e**i*a* (filling the last column); or

  ii the last tile could be *o*i*o**a* (in which case the two squares above or below this last tile must be filled with another horizontal tile).

In case **i**, before positioning the last tile, you must have tiled the first three columns – which can be done in R_3 different ways; in case **ii**, before positioning the last two (horizontal) tiles, you must have tiled the first two columns – which can be done in R_2 different ways.

$$\therefore R_4 = R_3 + R_2$$

The same reasoning shows that

$R_5 = R_4 + R_3$, $R_6 = R_5 + R_4$, and so on.

b Use the rule discovered in part **a** together with the fact that $R_1 = 1$, $R_2 = 2$ to work out how many different ways there are to tile a 2×20 rectangle with 2×1 tiles.

he numbers you have just calculated are called *Fibonacci numbers* – xcept that the Fibonacci numbers should really begin *one term earlier*.

'How many ways are there to tile a 2×0 rectangle?'

he (slightly unexpected) answer is '1 way': *sit tight and do nothing*. So the quence of Fibonacci numbers begins like this:

1, 1, 2, 3, 5, 8, 13, ...

ese Fibonacci numbers may not look very impressive, but they crop all over the place. The nth Fibonacci number is usually denoted by ; so $F_3 = 2 = R_2$. The last few problems introduce you to some of eir magical patterns. At this stage they can be no more than perimental observations: for proofs you must wait until book *ta* – the next book in this series.

7 a Write the first ten Fibonacci numbers, leaving a fair amount of space between successive terms.

Write the sum of the first *two* terms underneath the *second* term; write the sum of the first *three* terms underneath the *third* term; and so on up to the fifth term.

$$1 \qquad 1 \qquad 2 \qquad 3 \qquad 5 \qquad 8 \qquad 13 \qquad 21 \qquad 34 \qquad 55$$

$$1 = 1$$
$$1 + 1 = 2$$
$$1 + 1 + 2 = \underline{\quad}$$
$$1 + 1 + 2 + 3 = \underline{\quad}$$
$$1 + 1 + 2 + 3 + 5 = \underline{\quad}$$

The first two of these 'running sums' make it look as though the original sequence may be reappearing. The next few running sums force one to think again. But there is a sense in which the original sequence is hidden in these running sums. Can you see how?

b What do you expect the sum of the first six terms to be? Check your guess.

The next problem suggests that the behaviour you observed in problem 7 may arise because the sequence of Fibonacci numbers is in many ways like more familiar sequences of *o*e**.

8 a Write the first ten powers of 2 (starting with $2^0 = 1$) leaving plenty of space between successive terms.

Write the sum of the first *two* terms underneath the *second* term;
write the sum of the first *three* terms underneath the *third* term; and so on up to the fifth term.

$$2^0 = 1 \quad 2^1 = 2 \quad 2^2 = 4 \quad 2^3 = 8 \quad 2^4 = 16 \quad 2^5 = 32 \quad 2^6 = 64 \quad 2^7 = 128 \quad 2^8 = 256 \quad 2^9 = 512 \quad 2^{10} = 1024$$

$$1 = 1$$
$$1 + 2 = \underline{\quad}$$
$$1 + 2 + 4 = \underline{\quad}$$
$$1 + 2 + 4 + 8 = \underline{\quad}$$
$$1 + 2 + 4 + 8 + 16 = \underline{\quad}$$

What do you notice?

b What do you expect the sum of the first six terms to be? Check your guess.

9 Write the first ten Fibonacci numbers, leaving plenty of space between successive terms.

Write the sum of the *first and third* terms underneath the *third* term;
write the sum of *first, third and fifth* terms underneath the *fifth* term; and so on.

$$
\begin{array}{cccccccccc}
1 & 1 & 2 & 3 & 5 & 8 & 13 & 21 & 34 & 55
\end{array}
$$

$1 = 1$

$1 + 2 = 3$

$1 + 2 + 5 = \underline{}$

$1 + 2 + 5 + 13 = \underline{}$

$1 + 2 + 5 + 13 + 34 = \underline{}$

What do you notice? Can you explain?

10 a Write the first ten Fibonacci numbers, leaving plenty of space between successive terms.

Write the *sum of the squares* of the first *two* terms underneath the *second* term;
write the sum of the squares of the first *three* terms underneath the *third* term; and so on.

$$
\begin{array}{cccccccccc}
1 & 1 & 2 & 3 & 5 & 8 & 13 & 21 & 34 & 55
\end{array}
$$

$1^2 = 1$

$1^2 + 1^2 = 2$

$1^2 + 1^2 + 2^2 = \underline{}$

$1^2 + 1^2 + 2^2 + 3^2 = \underline{}$

It is not clear how to interpret the answers. 6 and 15 may not seem to be related to Fibonacci numbers – until you remember that you squared before adding, so you should not be surprised if the answers are **o*u*** of Fibonacci numbers:

$6 = 2 \times 3 = F_{\_} \times F_{\_}$; $15 = \underline{} \times \underline{} = F_{\_} \times F_{\_}$.

b What do you expect the sum of the squares of the first six Fibonacci numbers to be? Check your guess.